The Essence of Magick

A Wiccan's Guide to Successful Witchcraft

By Amaris Silver Moon

The Essence of Magick: A Wiccan's Guide to Successful Witchcraft
By Amaris Silver Moon

Copyright © 2014 Amaris Silver Moon

ISBN-13: 978-1500820480
ISBN-10: 1500820482

www.wiccanspells.info

This book is written to the best of the knowledge of Amaris Silver Moon. It is based on her experiences of magick, spells and reality creation. Since each reality is individual and subjective, Amaris cannot take responsibility for how you choose to use the information contained in this book, or the outcome of any spells you may cast.

All rights reserved. This book or any portion thereof may not be reproduced or exploited in any manner whatsoever without the express written permission of the publisher, except for the use of brief quotations.

Cover image: Celtic Pentagram by Cherrie Ann Button
http://cherrieb.redbubble.com

CONTENTS

	Introduction	5
1	Wicca: An Introduction	8
2	Understanding and Working with Energy	16
3	Daily Witchcraft – Transforming Each Moment	22
4	Essential Witchcraft Skills	29
5	The Witch's Tools	52
6	Living in Tune with Your Body	70
7	Spells and Rituals	78

~ Introduction ~

Merry Meet!

I was introduced to Wicca many years ago, back when I was a young girl living in the countryside. There, I had plenty of time and space to learn about and practice the Craft. I wasted no time in building my humble beginner's altar, which instantly became my own sacred space, and I was overjoyed to write and perform spells and rituals together with a close friend. We spent many a night beneath starry skies in the woods surrounding my childhood home, and celebrated the sabbats out in the fields. It was a very special time, when I strengthened my bond with magick.

I have always had a very strong connection with nature and Mother Earth, and would spend my days in the woods searching for fairies and gnomes or talking to trees. So naturally, Wicca made a lot of sense to me. Finally I had come across a community that honoured and celebrated nature in a way that resonated with me and my values, and a faith that allowed for magick.

I had always believed in spirits and otherworldly beings, no matter what my parents or teachers told me, and I knew in my heart that there was more to this world than meets the eye. I had a feeling that perhaps everything isn't as solid as it seems; maybe the universe is just a bit more malleable than traditional wisdom tells us – and perhaps we have a lot more power over our lives than we allow ourselves to believe.

Wicca provides ways to influence the course of our lives through spell work. What I didn't understand back then, however, was exactly *how* it all worked. I learned that spells, herbs and crystals all have different properties and purposes, but *how*?

Being a very curious and inquisitive person, I was never going to settle for simply casting spells and not understanding how they actually worked. So I set about a lifelong mission to try and understand the inner workings of the universe, the patterns of nature, and the principles behind the duality of the Goddess and God. I learned about philosophy, religion and science, studied the teachings of the Buddha, explored Hermetics and other magic systems, became acquainted with the functions of crystals and orgonite, practiced meditation and the Law of Attraction, read up on quantum mechanics and the Holographic Theory, and learned to perform energy healing and tai chi.

It seems the older I got, the more I was tuning in to the world of energy. It seemed to span all the belief systems I was drawn to, providing a logical system explaining pretty much everything. From quantum physics to reincarnation, from black holes to astral projection, from religious apparitions to dream interpretation – when viewed from an energy perspective it all made perfect sense to me.

Since creating my website (wiccanspells.info) I have received a myriad of questions from visitors about Wicca and spellcraft. The questions often relate to how they can best improve their chances of success at a certain spell, what to do if they don't have a specific tool or colour of a candle, and whether spells can be repeated or amended. I enjoy these conversations and they have touched and inspired me, and soon the idea for this book began to take seed in my mind.

With this book I want to share with you all that I have learned, and provide you with the knowledge to truly understand magick. With this knowledge you will increase your magickal skills and it will assist you in becoming the most powerful witch you can be.

What will this book give you?

This book provides you with a concise and practical approach to successful witchcraft through understanding and working with energy, as well as a cascade of spells, exercises and rituals. Each spell is accompanied by an information box explaining why the spell is constructed the way it is, in order to deepen your understanding of spell work and to help you amend or create spells as you please.

If you come across a spell which you feel would really help you, but you are lacking one or more of the 'ingredients,' I hope this will no longer deter you, but that instead you will have the means and resources to find out for yourself with what you may substitute the missing items.

There are endless opportunities all around us waiting to be grasped. Life is a beautiful manifestation of consciousness with which we can play and have fun, enjoying all the ups and downs of this colourful world, while learning how to find our highest path in order to live our ultimate existence.

Enjoy, and Blessed Be.

Amaris

CHAPTER 1

Wicca: An Introduction

Wicca takes many of its elements from ancient Celtic paganism and druidism, at a time when it was crucial for humans to live in harmony with nature. It is this harmony and balance that we as modern Wiccans seek to recreate.

Wicca as we know it was shaped in the twentieth century by people such as Gerald Gardner, often known as the father of the pagan renaissance. Gardner was a poet and historian who had a profound interest in druidic magick and Celtic paganism. In 1954, he published *Witchcraft Today*, a book which explored the application of witchcraft in the modern world. This book brought witchcraft out from the shadows and into the lives of spiritual seekers worldwide. Today the number of Wiccans is growing, with more and more people acknowledging our faith as a religion.

Key beliefs

Wicca is a spiritual way of life, where we strive to attain balance and harmony in ourselves and with the world around us. Wiccans live to honour nature and the divine that exists within each of us, with awe and respect for all beings. It is not a dogmatic religion; we have no commandments or rule books to follow, since we value free thought, will and personal responsibility. This is why Wicca is attractive to people who wish to forge their own spiritual paths.

There are a few key beliefs that are shared by most Wiccans, although the applications of them may differ from person to person. Remember, we all walk different paths. While it is good to seek inspiration from others, don't forget that you are the best teacher you will ever have.

The Goddess and God

Since Wicca is a religion of balance, we recognise both a male and a female deity. Everything that exists – all gods and goddesses, humans and animals, every inanimate object in our universe – comes from one source, Spirit. Spirit is the creative life force which forms the most basic building blocks of the Universe. However, this force has two polarities, and these are represented by the Goddess and God. The Goddess and God represent the ultimate balance and harmony of the universe, since their energies are opposite, but complementary.

The Goddess corresponds with the feminine energy present in all things. She is often represented by the Moon, and her energy is receptive, intuitive, contemplative and protective. Her creative power works by pulling things towards her, just as the Moon draws tidal waters toward itself.

The God corresponds with the masculine energy present in all things. Often represented by the Sun, his energy is active, expansive, focused and forceful. His creative power works by pushing his energy towards things. Think of the Sun beaming its rays onto Earth, causing plants to grow and people to thrive.

Goddess	**God**
Receptive	Active
Attracting	Projecting
Intuitive	Focused
Protective	Expansive
Contemplative	Forceful

We all contain both Goddess and God energy, and it is important to acknowledge and accept these energies within you; your personality and actions embody both Goddess and God energy. As an analogy, take the act of writing. In order to write about a subject, we must first receive information (by reading, listening to others, or even by just daydreaming). By receiving information, we are using Goddess energy. Now we take this information and project it onto a piece of paper or a computer screen. This forceful and direct act is an embodiment of God energy.

The Goddess and God have many different faces. For example, the Norse goddess Freya and the Egyptian goddess Isis are just two aspects of the same Goddess. We can invoke their many different aspects in order to create magick successfully (more about this in the chapter on invocation on page 42).

Harm None – The Wiccan Rede and the Threefold Law

A second universal aspect of Wicca is that of harming none. *The Wiccan Rede* is an ethical guideline that Wiccans adhere to, and it contains one of our governing principles: *"Eight words the Wiccan Rede fulfil: an' ye harm none, do what ye will."* Now, this doesn't mean that Wiccans are weak or turn the other cheek when someone harms them. What it does mean is that a true Wiccan takes responsibility for their actions and always considers what impact those actions may have on other beings.

Another part of the Rede is: *"What ye send forth comes back to thee."* Whatever energy you send out into the universe will come back to you. The wise Wiccan recognises that we are all interconnected. If you bless another person, you are also blessing yourself, and if you curse another person, you are cursing yourself. Nothing is without consequences, especially in magick.

As Wiccans, we need to learn how to live harmoniously with nature and other beings where we can. True Wicca is not about bending circumstances to your will – it is about working with the Divine Order, accessing a higher state of consciousness from where we can best attract the circumstances we want. In Wicca, we must first seek to change within before we can see changes without.

"Bide the Wiccan Law ye must,
In perfect love and perfect trust
Eight words the Wiccan Rede fulfil:
An' ye harm none, do what ye will.

What ye send forth comes back to thee
So ever mind the rule of three.
Follow this with mind and heart,
Merry ye meet, and merry ye part."

Living in tune with nature

A third universal aspect of Wicca is to live in tune with nature. We celebrate eight sabbats each year that reflect the cycles of nature, as well as the life cycle of the Goddess and God. By attuning to these cycles, we honour the passing of time whilst developing an understanding and acceptance of the fundamental truths of birth, life, death and re-birth.

The Divine exists in all things, and by connecting to it, we learn more about our true nature. You don't need to move to an isolated cottage in a forest to do this. Even city dwellers can take time to connect with nature. A simple thing such as growing potted herbs to use in your food (and rituals!) can connect you to the natural cycle of life.

Above and beyond acknowledging the sabbats and honouring the way of Mother Earth, it also involves living in tune with the energies that surround us. As I will explain fully later in this book, our whole world consists of an intricate web of energy that flows through and around us. This energy is the energy that gives life and form to everything that exists.

This is also the energy that we use in magick. The real art of magick is learning to recognise this energy, and to recognise its patterns. Witches don't force reality to bend to our wishes. Rather, we live and work with these energies so as to become one with their ebb and flow. In doing this, we find the paths of least resistance towards our truest desires. This is true magick, and it holds potentials for deep and profound spiritual growth.

The Wheel of the Year: The Eight Sabbats

The eight sabbats are festivals that Wiccans and other pagans celebrate to mark the seasons and honour the passing of time. They are times of celebration, reflection and worship, where we appreciate and attune to the cycle of nature and the changes in season. Because we are children of this Earth, her changes are also ours.

The circular nature of the Wiccan calendar reminds us that things come and go and then come again; it is birth, death and rebirth – the endless cycle of life.

There are four Lesser Sabbats that mark the solar phases of the year (two solstices and two equinoxes), and Four Greater Sabbats that celebrate fertility and agriculture. The Greater Sabbats are celebrated at the height of each season, when natural energies are at their peak.

Here is a brief look at each of them. (Please note that these dates apply to celebrations on the northern hemisphere – on the southern hemisphere the Wheel is reversed so that Yule happens on Litha and Ostara on Mabon.)

Samhain (31 October)

Samhain (in the West most commonly known as Hallowe'en) is the Witches' New Year. It marks the end of summer. The God now dies in order to be reborn again at Yule, while the Goddess carries the fire of the sun in her womb until spring. We celebrate the last harvest, before winter comes to clean the slate once more. It is a time for releasing the old, and cleansing to prepare for the new.

This is also a sabbat for honouring our dead and contemplating death. It is said that on this night the veil between this world and the next is the thinnest, and spirits come across to walk among the living. Many turn to the graves of loved ones to honour and remember them.

Yule (21-22 December – Winter Solstice)

Yule marks the shortest day of the year, and thus the return of the sun. The Goddess once again gives birth to the God, after which she will sleep until Imbolc, when she will awaken again as a young maiden.

This sabbat represents the battle between light and dark – the duality of life. They are now in perfect balance, before light returns once more, triumphing over death and darkness. Although that is not to say that the darkness is negative in that sense; light and dark complete each other and one cannot exist without the other.

Imbolc (2 February)

Imbolc marks the transition of the Goddess, who completes the circle as she shifts from a crone (the old Goddess) to a maiden (the young Goddess). The days are lengthening and the increasing light of the new-born God awakens her from her slumber. The world is born again, and the agricultural year begins as the first sprouts and buds appear on the face of the earth. We celebrate fertility and renewal.

This day is traditionally celebrated as the Day of Brighid (pronounced "Breed"), the Celtic Goddess of smith craft, poetry and medicine. She is the Triple Goddess – the Maiden, the Mother and the Crone – and we celebrate her in all her aspects.

This is a time for initiations, for plotting and planning for the year ahead now that spring is finally emerging and light returning.

Ostara (21 March – Spring Equinox)

Ostara (which Christians celebrate as Easter) is a time for fertility and childish wonder. The God is now a youth, preparing for manhood. The hare and eggs are symbols of fertility and abundance. Day and night are now equally long; it is a time of balance. From this point, the days will be longer than the nights and winter is officially over.

We celebrate the coming of spring by spending time in nature and watching the changes in the earth. We plant and bless seeds and prepare for the year ahead.

Beltane (30 April)

At Beltane, the God has reached manhood and the Goddess takes him as her lover, and from this sacred union all life emerges. It is a festival that celebrates the union of the masculine and feminine creative energies that have matured and now come together in perfect love and perfect trust. Fertility bursts forth from the shell that once contained it and the greenery of the Earth is fast returning.

Beltane is a fire festival, and people traditionally light bonfires and jump over fire to represent contact with the sun. It is a time for handfastings

(Pagan marriages), fertility rituals (such as erecting and dancing around the maypole); a time of joy and celebration of life. Rituals are often carried out to bless the crops for the coming summer.

Litha (21-22 June – Summer Solstice)

At Litha, Midsummer, the God is a middle-aged man at his peak, and we celebrate the light at its full power. From now on, the days will shorten and the light will wane. But on this night we celebrate the abundance of Mother Earth, and the Goddess is pregnant in preparation for delivering her fruits. It is a time for high magick and faery magick.

It is said that the faery folk are out doing mischief on this night, with the gate to their world opened to ours. Rituals relating to romance and love are aplenty at this time. It is also a time for celebrating existing love and renewal of vows. In the long days of summer we strive to spend more time outdoors and reconnect with nature, and on this day it is tradition to gather magickal and medicinal plants for drying and storing over winter.

Lughnasadh (1 August – also known as Lammas)

Lughnasadh marks the first harvest, and is a time of warmth and abundance. The God has placed his power in the grains, and as they are reaped his power diminishes. The work of spring and summer is finally paying off in the harvest, and we celebrate the fruits of the Goddess and God and spend this time focusing on gratitude and appreciation. It is tradition to make bread and sometimes to leave offerings of bread to the faeries.

The Celtic sun god Lugh gives name to this sabbat and, with the fading sun, some traditions commemorate his funeral on this day. Many will make wicker men at this time and burn them to symbolise the passing of Lugh. It is a time for letting go of old habits, and to release them you can write them down on a piece of paper which you place inside your wicker man before burning it.

Mabon (21 September – Autumn/Fall Equinox)

Mabon is the second harvest festival, and we celebrate the balance of the Goddess and God when once again the day and night are equally long.

We give thanks for the fruits of our labour and take some time to rest after the year's work. Warmth is behind us and cold lies ahead; we mourn the Sun God, but we also know that all things must come to an end and that this is a necessary part of life. After all, without endings there would be no beginnings.

On this sabbat we thank the Goddess and God for the bountiful harvest. We honour the changing of seasons and look back at the year that has passed, giving thanks to everyone and everything that helped us through it as we now bring it to a close.

CHAPTER 2

Understanding and Working with Energy

As a young beginner witch, I always worried that I would cast a spell wrong. And sure, it can go belly-up and backlash on you if you're not careful, but what I didn't realise back then was that with my eggshell approach I was blocking any positive changes that the spirits wanted to bring me. Radiating fear to such an extent will only serve to hinder developments in your life.

Later on, as I grew with age and experience, I came to understand that it is much more about the energy I emit before, during and after casting the spell, than about the words I say or the colour of the candle that I use. Our tools and the shapes, colours and symbols therein, all carry a certain vibration, and by choosing the appropriate herbs, stones, and colours, we use the tools as amplifiers, to extend our energy and to help us focus. But the main tool is us. It is you, the way you set your intention before the spell, the way you hold your energy while casting, and how you focus afterwards.

This is because – as many old religions and beliefs have held for millennia and which science is finally catching up with – we are all made of energy. Energy is our truest essence, and the essence of everything around us, from the tallest tree and the fastest jaguar to the smallest twig and the quietest stone. And behind the steering wheel controlling our energies are our thoughts and feelings.

This idea that we can affect the external world through our consciousness dates back at least as far as Hermetic teachings about magick and alchemy written in the 2nd and 3rd centuries BCE. *"As above, so below"* is one of the ancient maxims of Hermeticism, and it describes the idea that our external universe mirrors our internal state, and vice versa.

And now, in modern times, man has delved deeper into the truths of our existence, and broken open the smallest building stones only to find that, in fact, energy lies deeper than matter, and connects the physical world in an infinite web. Quantum physicists are slowly uncovering this truth as they conduct experiments in which particles that are vast distances away from each other still affect each other's behaviour. One particularly famous experiment – the double-slit experiment – showed that particles acted differently when they were being observed by the scientists. The mere act of observation altered the particles' behaviour, which shows that consciousness does have an effect on material objects.

Energy comes before matter – your body is simply a manifestation of your energy. You use your five senses to organise the world into forms, but beyond our physical senses there is a world vastly richer and more colourful than we could ever imagine; a world where everything is connected, where each thing is part of another in an immense mandala of souls and beings and thoughts, a beautiful fractal that carries on into eternity.

Resonance and dissonance

Energy bodies have a way of entraining to each other. Have you ever noticed how someone who is in a terrible mood can walk into a room and bring everyone down? Or the opposite, when someone who is beaming with joy can lift a whole room? When an energy body holds a strong enough vibration of any kind, all the energy around it will entrain to that stronger vibration, because there is an innate desire to *resonate*.

If there is dissonance – disharmony – it will feel very uncomfortable for everyone involved, like two violins playing in different keys. That is why it is so difficult to stay in a certain mood when someone is strong enough to bring you up or down. That is also why some people may make you feel uncomfortable for no apparent reason – if their energy cannot comfortably bring itself into resonance with yours, the result is a feeling of uneasiness or even distress.

Imagine that you are a cloud of energy floating through a world of yet more energy clouds, and everything around you is trying to resonate in harmony. This means that if you are holding a certain vibration, you are inevitably going to attract more of that same vibration. Things, people and circumstances of that frequency will gravitate towards you like asteroids to the sun. There is the saying, "it never rains but it pours." If one thing goes wrong, you will lower your energy frequency and start attracting more unfortunate events into your life. Similarly, think of when you first fall in love with someone. Suddenly the world is smiling at you, you rarely fall ill, and you walk through life on a cloud. When you are that happy and so strongly optimistic, more joy will drop into your lap before you know it. You are simply attracting more of the same.

Energy and spellcasting

If we want to see changes in our lives, spells are a great kick-starter, but they won't do the work for us. They are a way for us to communicate our desires to the Universe, but holding the right focus and energy are what can truly create miracles.

Spells aren't strict rules that must be followed down to the slightest detail; they are simply guidelines that you can tailor as you wish. I write my spells in a way that works for me, but that doesn't mean that they will speak to you in the same way. I encourage you to find your own way and, in order to cast spells most efficiently, to pay attention to your **intent, energy**, and **focus**.

Let's look at these three in detail.

Intent

Our *intent* is a powerful way to set our course through life. It's like looking at a map of endless possibilities, and drawing an arrow in a certain direction. We decide where we want to go, each moment of each day – we have so much more control over our lives than we realise.

Sometimes you get stuck on your path and feel like you're not moving anywhere. This is a frustrating situation, but one you can always break out of. The first step is to set your intent – something you can do any time you like: before casting a spell, before a major challenge, or in preparation of a big change. However, to integrate this practice into your daily life, I would also recommend that you set your intent every morning when you wake up, for example: *"Today I intend to feel good, to see the best in everything, to make the most of everything, and to be patient with myself if I fail."*

Before casting a spell, set your intent as clearly as you can. The Universe is listening, and it appreciates clear messages.

Energy

Now that you understand the basic workings of energy, you will see its importance in magick and the profound effects it has on the outcome of a spell. Imagine the spell as a container, which must be filled with your own energy. The container holds the shape of your wishes, and your energy attracts the results.

It is therefore important to cast a spell from a place of joy, trust, and excitement, since these higher vibrations will draw in results of the same frequency. Negative emotions during casting will block any positive results. If you find yourself feeling sad or anxious when you are about to cast a spell, use the emotional clearing exercises in Chapter 6 to raise your vibration in order to ensure that you are in the best possible mindset.

Focus

After casting a spell, your focus is very important – you will greatly improve your chances of success if you carry on holding a strong, high vibration in your everyday life. To do this, you will need to make the most of what you have and whatever comes to you. Let's say you want to buy a house, and you cast a spell for your dream home. If you also view your current living space in a positive way, by being thankful for whatever you have and focusing on any aspect of it that brings you joy, then you are swiftly moving towards the reality of having that dream home of yours.

This can seem tough at first, since your mind might have a tendency to wander back into old ways of thinking and acting, but it's just about forming new habits. Hang in there! Conscious efforts soon become subconscious routines, and this higher state of being will quickly become your new way of life.

Ask yourself in any situation, *"How I can make the best of this?"* That question will automatically increase your vibration and flow, since it points your focus towards a higher reality.
The four steps to successful manifestation

Some people talk about positive thinking being the only key to manifesting your desires, but it's not quite that simple. There are four key components to propelling your magick work into quick and wonderful manifestations, namely:

~ Positive expectations
~ Gratitude
~ Benevolence
~ Trust

Positive expectations: Begin by visualising what you desire. Let's say, for example, that you are about to cast a spell to find love. Imagine how it would feel to already have that love in your life. Forget about any insecurities, worries, or the patterns of your past. Focus solely on that feeling of already having this love. Go deep into that feeling. Is it butterflies? Joy? Excitement? Stability? Whatever feelings you desire for your future relationship, play with them now, make them yours, immerse yourself in these feelings. Know that they will come to you. Those are your positive expectations.

Gratitude: Now look at what you already have in your life. Perhaps not a lover, but maybe a close friend whom you love, a parent who cares deeply for you, or a pet that is dear to you – anything you can find that has already manifested in your life that you can be grateful for, find it and surround yourself with it. Radiate love and gratitude. Thank the Goddess and God. By feeling grateful for what we already have, we are sending high energy towards what we want. Gratitude is one of the highest vibrations available to humans, and it always pays off to bathe in it.

Benevolence: Next, know that you don't always have a say in the course of things. If you have your eyes on a particular person whom you would like to attract, but in fact this person is not what is best for you, or you are not what is best for them, then your Higher Self knows this and will try to guide you off that path. You can, if you wish, stubbornly remain on that route, and try to bend fate to happen how you want it to, but this will only backlash later.

We stand humble before the Universe and its divine plan. We can state what we wish, we can voice our desires, but cannot fool Fate. This is why we add the words *"for the highest good"* in any incantation or wish, so as to show our benevolence and to ensure that we do not interfere with free will or the higher order of things.

Trust: Finally, we must put our trust in the Universe. Once you have expressed your desire and cast your spell, and carried out your visualisation and energy work, all that is left is to *know* deep within yourself that the Universe will now bring what is best for you. You are not always able to see the bigger picture, so if something manifests in an unexpected way, receive it with open arms and trust that it is a step towards your highest possible path.

If you follow these four steps you will begin to manifest things faster than you could ever imagine. Walk your life's path with an open mind and a trusting heart, and you will make the most of this divine playground you are in.

Stay focused on what you want,
while making the most of what you have.

CHAPTER 3

Daily Witchcraft – Transforming Each Moment

If we are to be truly successful in our witchcraft, we must integrate magick and its mechanics into our everyday lives. The modern witch transforms each moment – we are continuously working with the world and the energies around us to create the life we want for ourselves. If we want to attract money, say, then we might cast a money spell, but the spell will bear no real substance without a change of attitude in our daily lives.

Energy follows thought – that is the golden rule. You always get more of what you focus on. Let's continue with our example of money: if you are constantly focusing on your lack of money and your financial worries, then that is what you will get more of. If, however, you instead focus on what you already have (a roof over your head, food on the table, somewhere safe to sleep), and optimistically approach future possibilities, then your focus has shifted from the problem to the solution. As such, a money spell will be significantly more successful if, both before and after the casting, you shift your focus towards abundance and gratitude.

So let's find out how to do that. Don't be disheartened if it feels tough at first, because lack is powerful and can be overwhelming. Be patient with yourself and the Universe – each baby step will bring you closer to your new reality.

Visualisation

"We all possess more power and greater possibilities than we realize, and visualizing is one of the greatest of these powers."

- Genevieve Behrend

"When you visualize, then you materialize. If you've been there in the mind you'll go there in the body."

- Dr Denis Waitley

There is a reason why visualisation is so prominent in spell work. When we visualise something, we get into the *feeling* of that something, and that feeling will shift your energies towards whatever it is you visualise and begin attracting it into your life. Imagine your focus as a powerful magnet – whatever you point it at will be pulled towards you. It is up to you to point it in a direction that is helpful to you.

How do we visualise?

By visualising I mean pretending, or fantasising – it's really not more complicated than that. It's about awakening your imagination and letting yourself run wild with your dreams. Conjure up images of your ideal life, or the perfect outcome to your current situation – remember, in your mind there are no limits! As you do this, you will notice yourself feeling increasingly excited and giddy – this is your energy field raising its vibration and aligning itself with a higher reality. Doesn't it feel good? If it feels *this* good, whilst simultaneously bringing you closer to your goals, surely you will want to do this as often as you can!

Aside from visualisation during spell work, you can play your pretend games whenever you want – in the shower, on your way to work, before you fall asleep... The more you do this, the sooner your desires will begin to manifest in your reality.

Most people are afraid of going too far in their fantasies, because they have "realistic" expectations and "know" their limitations. You couldn't fantasise about a house *that* big, that will never happen. No, you couldn't possibly play with the thought of being self-employed, it's just too difficult... Or is it?

No! Nothing is impossible. Yes, some situations may be difficult, but when you are in the flow and enjoying your journey, even difficulties are quite easy. You learn to appreciate obstacles because they teach you something. So don't be afraid to throw yourself completely into any crazy wild fantasy you can possibly imagine. Know that it doesn't matter *what* you are imagining, it's the *feeling* you get when you are imagining it, which will attract more of that feeling into your life – so make sure it's a good one!

Let's say money, for example. Imagine yourself in total abundance. Money is effortlessly flowing into your life. The trick is not to worry about the 'how' – that's up to the Universe to sort out for you. What you need to think about is the 'what'. What do you want? If you had lots of money, what would you do? Imagine that feeling of freedom, really immerse yourself in it. All your worries are washed away. Where would you go? What would you buy? How would you dress, behave, decorate your home? These feelings will soon translate into behaviours and patterns within you, and will create an abundant mindset which will soon bring prosperity into your life.

(Please note that when I'm talking about abundance, I do not mean greed – you can have you want but remember to remain within the realm of white magick and compassion. And on this subject, generosity is another trait that will help you draw more money into your life – the more you give, the more you get.)

We can never be sure what form our manifestations will assume. For example, you may visualise a particular job you would like, and then some other unexpected career opportunity presents itself. It may turn out that this other job is exactly what you needed, and will bring you the same feelings you held whilst visualising the other job. We can't see the bigger picture and must remain open and optimistic in our expectations while the Universe, with all its infinite wisdom, does all the mixing and matching. You simply need to follow your feelings and intuition – if it feels good, go with it. If it doesn't feel good, find something that does.

Create a notebook for your visualisation work, and start journaling as if you already had whatever it is you wish for – love, confidence, money, adventure, whatever it may be. Play with it in your book. Find pictures that remind you of your goals and stick them in. Take out your felt tip pens and really set loose. This is your playground – let your imagination run wild.

In a nutshell...

Find a positive focus, imagine your dreams, and keep that warm feeling inside you as often as possible. Hold it in your tummy, let it wash over you, become the feeling. The Universe will respond accordingly.

> *The feeling must come from within*
> *before it can be manifested without.*

Daily Gratitude

There is good reason why gratitude is such a popular self-help concept. It shifts your focus from *what you lack* to *what you have* – and we all have things to be grateful for in our lives. Most days I thank the Goddess and God for my hands, because I use them for everything I love doing – writing, crafts, art (and they're very useful during spell work!). That's a simple thing to start with.

Another thing which most of us take for granted is food. Think of how much effort has gone into each of your meals – the planting and reaping, the hunting and fishing, the transportation and cooking... Most of us simply gulp down our dinner so that we can get back to what we were doing. But food is our sustenance and should be treated with respect and gratitude.

Every time before you eat, bless the food by holding your hands over it and thanking everyone who was involved in making the meal come together – and with meat or fish, thank the animal for giving its life so that you may eat and continue your own life. (I know a chef who always does this while he cooks food, and people often tell him his food is the best they've ever tasted!)

I tend to integrate gratitude a lot in my magick. Whenever I address the Spirits, the Goddess and God, or my own guardian angels and guides, I always begin by expressing my gratitude for all that they have already brought me. By expressing this I show humility and benevolence, and it is always rewarded.

Anyone can benefit from keeping a gratitude journal. Every morning when you wake up, or every night before bed (or whenever feels good for you), take some time to write down the things you are grateful for. Write in some detail, since this is more engaging and will help you get deeper into the feeling. Throughout your day, remember to stop and notice the little things in your life, and thank the Goddess and God for them. This high-vibration state will open you up to new and higher realms, where you can get into the flow and find more and more possibilities every day.

Even if your current situation feels far away from your desired reality, remember that there is always something to be thankful for – it's just a matter of perspective. To begin seeking solutions and a path to a better life, ask yourself in every situation, *"What can I learn from this?"*

You can transform anything into gratitude. For example, if you're in debt, focus on the fact that someone has lent you the money so that you can have a roof over your head for the time being. If you're single, focus on the time you have for yourself and your hobbies. If you're unemployed, focus on the free time you have to find work or develop any money-making ideas (or just walk in the park and enjoy the sunshine) – you get the picture.

It can feel unnatural at first, to dig out something positive from the very things that are bringing us down, but trust me – it *can* be done and it's always worth it. Once you have found a small point of positive focus, hold on to that, point your magnet in that direction, and watch your life transform.

Mindfulness

Almost every spiritual teaching talks about the importance of mindfulness – and for good reason; we are here on Earth to experience this physical existence, and in order to do so fully, one must be present and mindful. That's not to say you can't daydream – by all means, do! But mindfulness is still an incredibly useful tool, and I will tell you why.

Mindfulness is a key player in the pursuit of happiness, not only because it allows you to be present in the moment in order to observe and appreciate it fully, but also because it promotes composure and focus when you are faced with problematic or stressful situations. When you are mindful you can deal with any situation that arises, because when you are fully present there is no room for anxiety or judgement.

In magick, mindfulness is a superpower. With a clear and present focus, there are no limits to how quickly your dreams can manifest. Without the distractions of a tangled mind, you can focus your energy wherever you wish, in the most positive and effective way.

I have written a spell called Be Here Now: Mindfulness Spell (on page 102) that will nudge you in the right direction, but it is also important to practice regularly in order to achieve the best possible results. Here are some simple everyday exercises you can practice whenever you wish.

Noticing your surroundings

Take a moment or two each day to stop and notice what's around you. Use your senses to experience the present. Look around you. What do you see? Then look beyond that – what do you see there? Notice the little things. What can you smell? What do you hear? Take note of all the different sounds you can hear at once. How does the air feel against your skin? Your feet against the ground? Feel your breath, gently going in and out, effortlessly sustaining your body. So easy, and so wonderful.

This exercise will also heighten your intuition and your psychic senses – the more you do it, the more sensitive you will become. Practice makes perfect!

Pulling in the tentacles

Most of us have countless thoughts zooming through our heads at any given moment – what happened at work today, what will happen tomorrow, what to pick up for dinner tonight, the status of your bank account, and did you remember to pay those bills? It's incredible how much information we are processing constantly and incessantly – no wonder mindfulness is such a popular tool; give your brain a break once in a while!

I often imagine my thoughts as big tentacles or antennae springing out of my head, reaching into the past and into the future – worries, anxieties, anticipations, projects. Can you picture them now, the tentacles coming out of your head? Try to feel them, how far they reach, how many there are. Now take a deep breath and *pull them all in*. Literally imagine sucking them back into your head as you breathe in – bring them all back home. Then breathe out and relax. Do you feel different?

You don't need to always be thinking about and worrying over these things. You only ever need to deal with the present moment (unless you are constructively using your mind for planning or preparing). Notice how clear and light you can feel when you pull those tentacles in and leave the past behind you and let the future come in its own time.

Mindful tooth brushing

This could be done with any activity, but I've chosen tooth brushing because that's the sort of thing that most of us do on autopilot while we send our brains off into the ether. Instead, try to be fully present whilst brushing your teeth. Feel the brush against your teeth and gums, pay particular attention to each individual tooth, feel your weight pulling you towards the earth, your feet flat against the floor. Notice the temperature in the room, the lighting, the taste of the toothpaste. No doubt after this you will feel calmer and more present in your body and in the moment – and your teeth will probably feel cleaner than usual, too!

Magick in each moment

Remember that magick is everywhere, and that you are constantly creating the life around you. By following some or all of these exercises, you will heighten your senses and energies and begin to walk the path towards your highest possible existence.

> *"What we are today comes from our thoughts of yesterday, and our present thoughts build our life of tomorrow. Our life is the creation of our mind."*
>
> - Buddha

CHAPTER 4

Essential Witchcraft Skills

The previous chapter showed you how to shift your focus and raise your vibrations in your daily life, so as to continuously transform yourself and your life and create your highest reality. This chapter will cover some essential skills that will help you immensely in your witchcraft, such as working with energy and elements, casting a circle, and invoking deities to assist in your magick.

Working Directly with Energy

To become adept at spellcraft we must learn how to manipulate and focus energy, as well as balance our own energy fields. When energy flows through us unobstructed, we feel healthier, happier and calmer. We also increase our ability to focus our minds at any one task.

There are many things you can do to improve the energy flow in your body. Exercises like tai chi and yoga are very beneficial, and even simple things like taking daily walks will help. You can work with crystals and herbs that dissolve energy blockages and entrain your energy body to their healing frequencies. But as a Wiccan, you shouldn't stop there. The following exercises will teach you how to manipulate the flow of energy in your body. This helps you direct energy where it needs to go during spellcasting. Anyone can learn to do this, but it may take some practice to become skilled at it.

The most effective way to manipulate energy is through your breath. Most esoteric teachings tell us that our breath is our connection to our Divine Source. When you breathe in, you absorb energy from your environment, and when you breathe out, you direct it where it needs to go.

Energy follows thought

To direct energy, all you need to do is focus on where you want it to go. Try this simple exercise to get a taste of how it works:

Sit in a comfortable position and calm your mind by taking ten deep breaths. When you feel calm and focused, take another deep breath in and imagine that you are breathing in the energy contained in the air around you. As you breathe out, focus on your thumb. Do this a few times. You will feel a sensation, usually a warm tingling. This is the energy being concentrated in your thumb – you are directing it there with your mind!

Once you have felt this, you can play around with the energy. When I was first learning how to work directly with energy, one of my favourite things to do was to make an energy ball.

Making an Energy Ball

To make an energy ball, have your palms face each other about 20-30 centimetres apart. Take some time to ground and center yourself. Now breathe in, and imagine your whole body absorbing energy from the air and from the earth. As you breathe out, focus on your palms and imagine the energy shooting out through them. Feel the energy forming a swirling ball. Remember, energy follows thought, so your visualisation is in fact creating real effects.

If you are a visual person you can picture the ball in front of you, and make it any colour or texture you want. You can play with the ball using your imagination – try, for example, visualising waterfalls or tornadoes surging out through your hands. Picture a thriving forest or jungle in your ball, or sparkles or bolts of lightning. Try filling it with sounds like your favourite music or the howling of wolves. Any image or feeling you can conjure up will help fill the ball with energy, since you are placing your focus (and thus your energy) within it.

Now try pushing your hands slightly closer together. You should feel the energy push against your hands. If you pull your hands further apart, you will feel a pulling sensation and the intensity will diminish. Practice pushing your hands towards and away from each other several times until you get a sense of how the energy ball feels.

You can use these energy balls in your magick. They are a powerful way of concentrating your energy, and since you can fill it with anything you want, you can create different balls for all kinds of purposes. One way to do it is to build up your energy ball until it feels strong, and then mentally place your desired outcome within the ball and carry on sending energy into it. Another is to build up the ball, and once you feel satisfied you can release the ball into the Universe with an incantation or prayer; or you can throw the ball towards a symbol, photograph or anything else that represents your dream.

Centering, Grounding and Shielding

Everyone who wants to be successful at witchcraft should take time to practice the arts of centering, grounding and shielding. This will improve your ability to focus your energies during spellcasting, which will lead to better results and more successful magick, but it will also help you in your day-to-day life.

Practicing these three skills can make a huge difference in the way you feel. You will be less affected by negative people or energies that surround you; you will feel calmer and more stable, and your connection to your Divine power will strengthen.

So, as you can see, it's a good idea to not just use centering, grounding and shielding when doing spells, but to integrate them into your daily life. At first, you might need to set aside a dedicated period of time each day for your practice, but it will soon become second nature. Eventually, you will be able to quickly and easily center, ground and shield yourself in any situation.

Centering

When casting a spell, you need to be able to put all of your focus on it. This is virtually impossible to do if you are not centered.

Whenever you put your attention somewhere, you are sending out a tendril of energy towards that something. Centering is the art of pulling these tendrils back in and balancing yourself within your core. It also helps you in day-to-day life since you will be more present in everything that you do.

To center yourself, you draw all your energy towards your spiritual center, by placing your full attention in that area. Traditionally, this is at the point just behind your navel, but you can also focus on your solar plexus or heart area. Play around with it and see what feels most comfortable to you.

Close your eyes and breathe deeply. Imagine that you are breathing in white, cleansing energy, and breathing out all the stress and tension in your body. As your body begins to relax, visualise a glowing ball of energy in your spiritual center, almost like a small sun – joyful, warm and revitalising. This is your place of personal strength and power. Put all your focus on this ball, and let your thoughts quieten as you feel its energy becoming stronger. If you are a visual person, you can see it glowing brighter and brighter. I am mostly kinaesthetic, so I tend to feel the ball getting warmer until this warmth spreads throughout my body.

This centering exercise can also be useful if you are feeling stressed or overwhelmed, or if you need to concentrate on one task.

Grounding

Grounding is essentially connecting you to Mother Earth's energies. If you are feeling scattered, or you are spending a lot of time in your head, grounding can help you feel stable and calm. If you cast a spell without being grounded, you could deplete your own energies. Grounding before casting will ensure that you draw energy from the earth to sustain you throughout the ritual.

Walking barefoot on soil is a quick and easy way to ground yourself, but this is not always possible or practical. Instead, we can connect to the Earth through our minds.

Sit or stand with your feet flat against the ground. Breathe deeply and slowly until you feel a calm come upon you. Now shift your attention to your feet and legs. Imagine them as trunks of a tree, strong and stable. Feel your energy extend beyond your feet and into the ground, as if you were growing roots reaching deep into the Earth. As you breathe in, visualise the Earth energy flowing into your roots and upwards into your body, filling and nourishing your entire being. Feel yourself connecting with the ancient energy of Mother Earth. As you breathe out, breathe into your roots, spreading and extending them even further. Continue doing this for several minutes – you will feel more solid and relaxed as you carry on.

If you ever feel weakened, ill or emotionally distressed, grounding yourself will stabilise and strengthen you.

Shielding

Have you ever been out in a public space and felt a sudden emotion – perhaps irritation or sadness – without knowing why? Humans are empathic beings and we subconsciously pick up emotions from people around us. We can use centering and grounding to help us feel better after we have been affected, but to stop it happening in the first place, we should learn how to *shield*.

Shielding is a skill that is beneficial to everybody, but especially to those who are sensitive to energy. Since practicing witchcraft tends to increase our energy sensitivity, this should be one of the first things you learn how to do in order to protect yourself. It is a method of clearly defining your own personal energetic space and limiting the influence of others upon it. It can also be used against non-human entities.

You should center and ground yourself before setting up your shield. Once you have done this, visualise a protective barrier around you. My shield is usually about an arm's length from my body, but this can vary depending on whether I am in a crowded space or not. Choose a distance that feels comfortable to you.

Shielding techniques vary. One popular method is to visualise a reflective shield, like a large glass egg, around your body. This shield will reflect back any negative energies and only let positive energies pass through. I like to visualise a shimmering white light around my body. This white light has a very high vibration, and only lets in energies of similar frequencies. Play around with colours and see what feels best to you.

Breathing is another way of balancing and strengthening your aura. Use deep, focused breaths to conjure up a strong, protective shield around you. Throughout the day, take a few strong breaths to connect with and replenish your shield.

You can also make your shield stronger by asking your spirit guides to surround you with their protective light.

Once your shield is created, know that no negative energies can pass through it. They may be reflected back to their source, or they may dissipate, and you will be safe and protected.

Working with the Elements

Air, water, earth, fire – the four elements are representations of the four most basic energy patterns that exist in our Universe. All that is contains the four elements. All humans, plants, animals, minerals – even emotions and thoughts – are made up of combinations of these elements.

Earth is the energy pattern of stable growth, nourishment, grounding and physical manifestation. When the energy of Earth flows freely through you, you feel nourished, sustained and stable. A good representation of Earth is a big sturdy oak tree. It grows slow but steady. It draws nourishment from the soil, and in turn releases nourishment into the atmosphere in the form of oxygen.

Earth corresponds with North, the colour green, and the pentacle.

Air is the energy pattern of communication, perception, thought and breath. When the energy of Air flows freely through you, you are perceptive and clear-minded. Air represents interconnectedness and links all beings. Wind is the purest physical representation of Air, constantly flowing and bringing renewal and fresh energies.

Air corresponds with East, the colour yellow, and the wand.

Fire is the energy pattern of creation, transformation, passion and change. When the energy of Fire flows freely through you, you embrace change in your life. You transform yourself, and you are constantly creating (this can refer to physical creation, as well as mental or emotional creation). Physically, fire is a destructive force, but it is also one of the purest representations of transformation.

Fire corresponds with South, the colour red, and the athame/sword.

Water is the energy pattern of flowing, cleansing, healing and openness. When the energy of Water flows freely through you, you are open and non-resistant. Think of a river or a stream, where the water flows around any obstacles, always finding the path of least resistance. It also represents the ever-changing nature of life, and inspires us to gracefully accept and adapt to these changes.

Water corresponds with West, the colour blue, and the chalice.

Wiccans also recognise a fifth element, known as **Spirit**. This is essentially the energy I am talking about in this book – the glue that holds everything in the Universe together. It represents consciousness, union, and the energy of the Goddess and God.

Why work with the elements?

The elements are very important archetypes in pagan traditions worldwide. When we work with the elements, we learn to distinguish these four energy patterns both in the natural world and in ourselves. They help us understand ourselves and our environments better, and they also help us truly see that everything is interconnected, since the same four basic energies run through everything that exists.

One of the best ways to communicate with our Higher Self is through symbols (since they can hold, through association, more information than words alone). The four elements are powerful symbols to call on, since they can be used as representations for every energy pattern that exists.

When we cast a circle, we usually call on all the elements. By doing this, we are drawing on universal energy in its four purest forms. It is a way of connecting fully to the world around you, which raises more energy for your intent. Calling on the four basic symbols of energy and feeling them embody you is a powerful way to connect with your Higher Being.

The elements within us

We all contain embodiments of the four elements, but we will usually not have an equal balance of all four. As Wiccans, inner element work is a good way to balance aspects of your personality and become more stable and integrated.

For example, if you are determined and stubborn, you likely have a lot of Earth in your personality. Stubbornness and determination can be useful, but they can also lead to frustration when things don't go your way. In that case, you could work with Water in order to learn how to flow around obstacles instead of trying to move them with sheer determination.

When I was younger, my Water, Air and Fire elements were balanced, but I had very little Earth energy in me. This meant that I didn't really feel connected to the physical world and I was always daydreaming. Practical matters bored and exhausted me, and my financial situation was less than stable. Once I learned how to work with the elements within myself, I took time to meditate on Earth energy, calling it into my life as often as possible. After a while, I felt much more balanced – and while I will always have an affinity for daydreaming, it won't get in the way of the practical matters of my life.

A quick way to find out what elements influence you the most is to have a natal astrological chart drawn for you – you could get an astrologer to do this for you, but there are many places to do this online for free. The elements are an important part of astrology, and you will be able to see which elements are strong in your chart, and which are weak.

Another way to do this is to simply make a list of all your personality traits that you can think of. You won't be able to think of everything at once, so give this project a few days, or even weeks. Write down every aspect of yourself that you can think of, both positive and negative.

After you are done, assign an element or two to each trait. Here are a few examples:

> I am a good communicator (Air)
> I sometimes overanalyse things (Air)

When I start a task, I always finish it (Earth)
I can be quite stubborn about getting my way (Earth)
I often know what other people are feeling before they even say a word (Water)
I sometimes get caught up in my emotions (Water)
I often get new ideas that I feel really passionate about (Fire)
I sometimes find it hard to control my temper (Fire)

You will begin to understand which elements runs strong in your personality and which ones you could use more of. In order to balance yourself, meditate on the energy of the elements which you feel you lack, which will call their energies into your life.

I have adapted this process from *Initiation to Hermetics*, a manual for beginner magick written by Franz Bardon who, though not a Wiccan, was a very powerful and influential 20th century magician. He felt that in order to practice magick, one should have a balanced personality and not lack or have an excess of any of the four elements.

Element Meditation

In order to learn more about the elements, you can meditate on their qualities. This exercise will help you connect to each element. If you find yourself lacking one or more of the elements you can focus specifically on those.

You will need:

Earth: A tree, a potted plant, a crystal, or a rock
Air: A stick of lit incense
Fire: A candle
Water: A bowl or chalice of water

Earth:

If you have a stone or crystal, hold it in your hands and feel its solid energy. Meditate on the stability of Earth and the physical manifestation of all things. If you are using a tree or plant, hold your hands on either side of it and feel its energy of growth and perfect health. Imagine the roots firmly planted in the soil, constantly drawing in the earth's nutrients. Contemplate nature's eternal balance, and imagine yourself firmly planted on the ground, your roots seated deep within Mother Earth.

Remember that you have a place on this earth, that you belong here and have a purpose in this life. You are the child of the ever-expanding branches of humanity, the endless tree of life that grows and spreads, and connects you to your ancestors all the way back to the beginning of time.

Say: *"I accept and invite Earth as part of my being, and ask that its divine properties be integrated into my soul."*

Air:

Light the incense and watch the smoke rise. Hold your hands in it, feel its scent, allow it to immerse you. Watch the swirling patterns it makes as it blends with the air around it. Reflect upon the way air carries sounds and communication, and connects all living beings. Visualise winds blowing within you, from light and playful gusts to powerful storms, reviving you and bringing you clarity and renewal.

Know that all life is interconnected. You are separate from no one; rather, you are an integral part of the great web of life. You are creativity and intelligence embodied, and you have the gift of communication with which you can connect to other beings and convey your thoughts and ideas. For each breath you take, you draw in fresh energy that renews your being.

Say: *"I accept and invite Air as part of my being, and ask that its divine properties be integrated into my soul."*

Fire:

Light the candle and watch the flame. Hold your hands on either side of it and feel the heat generated from the fire as it converts oxygen to carbon dioxide. Meditate on transformation, and the cycle of destruction and creation. Feel Fire's force, determined to get to where it's going, shying away from nothing and no one.

There is powerful courage and vigour within you. Confidence and strength triumph over fear and doubt. You can take whatever situation you come into and transform it for your highest good. You understand that the end of one thing means the beginning of something else, and you welcome change with enthusiasm and curiosity.

Say: *"I accept and invite Fire as part of my being, and ask that its divine properties be integrated into my soul."*

Water:

Gaze at the water and its calm surface. You were once surrounded by water, safe within the womb, and you will always be connected to it. Dip your hands in it and feel its refreshing coolness and softness. Water corresponds with deep wisdom, perception and insight. Become one with its fluidity and gentle motion. Feel it flowing within you, healing and rejuvenating you.

Your emotions are true messengers and guides in your life. You can come in contact with them and learn from them any time you wish; there is nothing to fear. You have the gift of empathy and compassion that allows you to connect with and understand yourself and all life. Any time you wish, you can enter into a state of flow and follow the path of least resistance.

Say: *"I accept and invite Water as part of my being, and ask that its divine properties be integrated into my soul."*

Casting a Circle

Casting a circle of protection is a way for Wiccans to protect themselves during magick work. It creates a high-energy space where you can safely carry out your magick, without the interference of any negative or harmful entities that might otherwise be attracted to your metaphysical energies during rituals and spell casting.

Marking out your circle

First, you want to decide where to create your circle. Whether you have an altar or just a peaceful corner of your home – or maybe outside in nature – pick a place where you are undisturbed so that you can focus and work in peace.

It's not necessary to mark out your circle, but some like to do it for ritual purposes, or for protection. You can, for example, create a circle of rocks or crystals, sprinkle sea salt or herbs along the edges of your circle, or place candles at each of the four cardinal points (West, North, East, and South – also representing the Four Elements.)

The next step is to conjure the pure energy that will surround and protect you. There are as many ways to do this as there are Wicca practitioners, so feel free to experiment until you find a way that is suitable to you and your practices.

How to cast a basic circle

Here is an example of a basic circle casting which can be performed quickly and easily without the use of tools.

Stand in the middle of your circle. Relax and breathe deeply. Imagine that your crown (the top of your head) opens up like a funnel to receive divine, white light. Your crown is always connected to the divine and to your Higher Self, and you can open up and amplify this channel at your will.

Open your arms, palms facing out. With each in-breath, visualise yourself pulling down pure, divine light through your crown, and as you breathe out, channel this light down your arms and out through your palms to create a protective shield around you. As you fill the circle with this high-vibration energy you may feel a tingle or buzz, a warm sensation, or feel light and uplifted.

Now hold one arm outstretched (the one you write with) and point to the edge of the circle. Spin around clockwise three times, mentally marking out your circle with the divine light. Then raise your arms above your head and say:

"I ask that the Goddess and God bless this circle
So that I may be free and protected within this space
Thank you – so mote it be"

You are now ready to cast your spell or perform your ritual.

To close your circle, hold out your arm and spin around anti-clockwise three times and feel the protective light dispersing. Thank the Spirits for their presence and declare the circle closed.

How to cast an advanced circle

This is an example of a more advanced circle ritual, for which you will need a compass and four candles. To direct the energy, use an athame or wand if you have one. If not, your index finger will suffice.
You can use white candles, or coloured candles for each point:

North – Green
East – Yellow
South – Red
West – Blue

Use the compass and place the candles at each of the cardinal points.

Light the North candle and say:

"Guardians of the North, Element of Earth
I call upon thee to be present during this ritual
Please join me now and bless this circle"

Light the East candle and say:

"Guardians of the East, Element of Air
I call upon thee to be present during this ritual
Please join me now and bless this circle"

Light the South candle and say:

"Guardians of the South, Element of Fire
I call upon thee to be present during this ritual
Please join me now and bless this circle"

Light the West candle and say:

"Guardians of the West, Element of Water
I call upon thee to be present during this ritual
Please join me now and bless this circle"

Now take your wand or athame and point it to the edge of the circle. Spin around clockwise three times, and visualise a bright white light entering you through your crown. Direct this light out through your arm, down through your tool and out to form the edge of your circle.

Then stand in the middle, and feel this white, divine light filling the circle and immersing your entire being. Say:

"Goddess and God, Guardian Angels, and Spiritual Guides
Please be present with me during this ritual
Bless this circle and keep me protected
No unwanted entities are welcome here
Only pure, divine beings are invited into this space
The circle is cast
So mote it be"

You are now ready to cast your spell or perform your ritual.

To close your circle, take your wand or athame and spin around anti-clockwise three times and feel the protective light dispersing. Thank the Spirits and Elements for their presence and declare the circle closed.

Invocation

Spirits, gods, goddesses and other entities

Otherworldly entities. How do they exist? Where do they come from? And how can we access their timeless wisdom and power?

Protective light

Bright white light has a high vibration and provides a strong protective field around you. To protect yourself with this light, visualise it surrounding you, immersing you, shining from a bright source deep within you or from a celestial space above you. Feel it reaching at least an arm's length away from your body. Keep visualising this bright field around you as you carry out your invocation, confident in the knowledge that nothing harmful can penetrate your luminous shield.

You can fortify it by saying the following words:

"Bright white light surrounds me
Divine light immerses me
I stand within its protective shield
And nothing can harm me"

Breathing

A sure way to raise your vibration is with deep, conscious breathing. Our breath is our connection to the divine, the ebb and flow that keeps us alive, and taking full, deep breaths will balance and strengthen your energy field.

More than once I have found myself floating in the vague world between sleep and wakefulness and felt a presence less than friendly attempting to latch onto me, but if I manage to breathe deeply I push these presences away. If you hold a strong enough vibration, nothing of a lower frequency can attach itself to you.

Breathe deeply into your stomach whilst performing your magick, and especially if you feel a negative presence approaching you.

Crystals

For extra protection, you can wear or carry gemstones or orgonite with protective qualities, for example black tourmaline, amethyst, hematite or jasper. You will find more information about crystals and orgonite in Chapter 5.

Banishing

If, despite all your efforts to protect yourself, you find that an unwanted presence is lingering in your home or your mind after you finish your magickal work, immediately cast the Banishing Spell under Spells and Rituals.

Example invocation

The first thing you must do when you want to invoke a being is to decide which one to call upon. For millennia, humans have summoned deities to assist with various purposes. Below, I have listed a few examples of beings from different cultures and faiths. As long as you treat them with respect and care, you are free to summon anyone you wish.

Entity	**Faith**	**Attributes**
Hecate	Greek	Crossroads, witchcraft, sorcery, knowledge of herbs
Freya	Norse	Life and death, fertility, female sexual empowerment
Odin	Norse	War and battle, wisdom, magic, poetry
Vishnu	Hindu	The creator and destroyer of all existences; governs, sustains and preserves the Universe and all the elements therein
Ganesh	Hindu	Beginnings and new endeavours, arts and sciences, removing obstacles
Isis	Egyptian	Motherhood, magic and fertility
Diana	Roman	Hunt, wild animals and woodland, ability to talk to animals
Neptune	Roman	Freshwater and the sea, horses and horseracing
Eros	Greek	Love, passion
Brighid	Celtic	Poetry, arts and crafts, medicine, fire
Vesta	Roman	Goddess of home and family
Cernunnos	Celtic	The Horned God, nature and fertility

| Ishtar | Babylonian | War, love, sex and fertility |
| Kuan Yin | Buddhism | Compassion and kindness, clairvoyance, musical abilities, protection, spiritual enlightenment |

If you want to know more about any of the above there is plenty of information online, where you can also learn about other spiritual beings that might better fit your purpose.

Apart from gods and goddesses you can also invoke the Four Elements, your Higher Self, a passed friend or relative – anyone you wish to summon. Call them with humility and respect, and they will join you.

Now take the following skeleton of an incantation below, and rewrite it to suit your desires. Then read it out when standing in your circle.

Write your incantation from the suggestion below. We do this in three parts. First, we want to connect with the soul we are calling:

"I call upon thee, [Name]
To join me in my circle of light
To accompany me in this ritual"

Then we must ensure that we are not inviting any impostors:

"No traitors or tricksters are welcome here;
Only the true soul and spirit of [Name]"

And finally we want to state our purpose for calling them:

"Please share with me your [protection/wisdom/guidance/advice etc]
So that I may [learn/grow/gain… etc]
I am forever grateful for your assistance
May we all be forever blessed
So mote it be"

When you are done, remember to send them home by saying the following:

"Thank you, [Name], for your presence and assistance

Go back whence you came, go in peace
Any energy that isn't mine, I release now
So mote it be"

Afterwards, ground yourself and then close your circle.

Divination

What is Divination?

The word "divination" comes from the Latin word *divinatio*, which means the gift of prophecy.

Seen from an energy perspective, divination is simply the act of tuning into and recognising the energy patterns that are occurring in your life (or someone else's) at the present moment. We can see which energy patterns are holding us back, which ones have potential for us, and what we should focus on in order to achieve our desires.

When we divine, we are not predicting the future, because the future is always fluid. We can, however, predict a most likely outcome based on the path we are presently on. We can also heed warnings from divination, and change our paths in order to avoid certain outcomes.

Energy patterns can always be influenced. If you see, at the time of the reading, that the path you are on now will lead to a certain outcome, then you can change that path. Divination can help you make better choices and learn how to work with the Universe by deepening your understanding of the options and potentials in your life.

There are many different ways to divine, but ultimately all these ways are just different tools to help us connect with our Higher Self – the part of us that has a deep knowledge of the energy patterns surrounding us.

A good way to communicate with our Higher Self is through symbols. Symbols are a great way to translate energy patterns into a language that we can easily understand. Symbols contain much more information than words do, and they can evoke powerful feelings and associations. This is why many divination systems, such as runes, the tarot and the I Ching are based on the use of symbols and archetypes.

Everyone has the innate ability to connect with their Higher Self. Divinatory tools are not strictly necessary for this purpose, but they are a very useful training wheel, because they help us to become sensitive to energy patterns. As you get more practice in the arts of divination, you will find that your intuition and psychic abilities develop. Some people eventually stop using their tools and start divining by direct methods instead, such as clairvoyance or channelling, speaking directly to their Higher Self and their guides.

In short, divination will help you strengthen your inner guidance, and you will find that your line of communication with your Higher Self and your spirit guides will be much clearer.

Divination Methods

Here are four popular divination methods that I have found to be useful:

Tarot cards

The tarot is a deck of cards that originated in Italy in the 15th century. Originally it was used for playing card games, but it later turned into a divinatory tool. The tarot contains 78 cards split into two categories – the Major Arcana and the Minor Arcana.

The Major Arcana consists of 22 cards, and each card represents a theme or aspect on our path to spiritual growth. These cards show us the dominant energy patterns which are occurring in our lives.

The Minor Arcana consists of 56 cards, divided into four suits that correspond with the four elements – cups (water), wands (fire), swords (air) and pentacles (earth). While the Major Arcana deals with our underlying spiritual themes, the Minor Arcana shows us the energy patterns occurring in our day-to-day lives.

Runes

Runes are the letters of an ancient alphabet which was used by Nordic peoples up until the Middle Ages. The legend goes that Odin, the all-knowing father of the Norse gods, brought the wisdom of the runes back from the afterlife after performing a self-sacrificial ritual.

The word "rune" translates roughly as "secret" or "hidden wisdom", and while each rune represents a letter of the alphabet, they are also powerful symbols that can be used for divination or magick.

It is fairly easy to make your own set of runes. My first set consisted of twenty-four pebbles that I had collected on the beach, each of similar shape and size. I used acrylic paint to mark each pebble with a rune. You can also carve the runes into small bits of wood.

I Ching

The I Ching is a divination system derived from an ancient Chinese text of the same name. The I Ching is considered to be a practical guide to daily life, and it is based on the principles of Yin and Yang – female and male energy. According to the I Ching, every situation in life can be interpreted as a specific interaction of Yin and Yang energies.

There are sixty-four different symbols in the I Ching, and each is made up of a six-lined figure of broken and unbroken lines, otherwise known as a hexagram. Traditionally, these hexagrams are determined by throwing coins or yarrow sticks on the ground.

Pendulum

A pendulum is not a symbolic divination system like the previous three. Instead, it is a way of using your body as a medium of communication with your subconscious mind and Higher Self. A pendulum consists of a piece of string with a weight at the end of it. You can buy a ready-made pendulum, or make one yourself with string and a small object such as a ring that you can tie to the end of the string.

To use a pendulum, hold the end of the string between your fingertips while keeping your hand as relaxed as possible. The pendulum moves in different ways to give yes-or-no answers to the questions you ask it. Sometimes the pendulum will swing from side to side, and sometimes it will swing in a circle. To determine which movements mean "yes" and which mean "no", start off by asking questions that you already know the answers to.

Preparing Yourself for Divination

Whichever divination method you use, it's important to be in the right state of mind so that you can receive clear and accurate answers. It's also important to connect with your medium of divination. When I buy a new set of tarot cards, I like to sit with them for a while and infuse them with my energy until I feel a strong connection with them. I also do this every time before using the cards.

Method:

First of all, **ground and center** yourself.

Now, hold your divination tool in your hand and relax. As you breathe in, feel yourself pulling in the energies of your tool, and as you breathe out, feel your own energies flowing down through your arms and out into the tool. Do this back and forth (or in a clockwise circle, going in through your right arm and out through your left) until you feel like your two energies have merged. You and your divination tool are ready to begin.

Say:

"I am open to receive the answers to my queries."

Now ask your question. Keep it focused yet not too detailed. You can also ask generally about your current situation or an upcoming project, without having a specific question in mind. Your Higher Self will then communicate to you where you currently stand in that situation.

Keep a relaxed and present mind while divining. If you try to force it you will immediately block the messages from coming through to you. Remain open and analytical, and enjoy the process. If you receive an answer you are unsure of (such as a tarot card you can't interpret or a rune you don't know the meaning of), have a look online.

CHAPTER 5

The Witch's Tools

Are Tools Necessary?

Tools are never absolutely necessary for magick, but they can be very helpful, especially for the beginner. They focus our thoughts and emotions (i.e. our energy), which is where the true magick lies. Each tool is dedicated to a specific magickal purpose, and it is thus effective at directing energy according to that purpose. We have talked before about how everything is made up of energy. Each tool has its own unique energy frequency, depending on its shape and the material it is made of – but most importantly, the energy we imbue it with. That is why a simple letter opener can make a powerful athame for a Wiccan who is skilled at energy work.

For beginners, it is a good idea to make your own tools – at least some of them. Creating something helps you connect with it, and if you are focused on the magickal purpose of your tool while making it, you will infuse it with that energy. It will also help you forge a stronger connection with your tool. I have included some helpful ideas for DIY Wiccan tools in the next chapter.

You can also buy your tools should you wish. There is a huge variety of beautiful tools available online, and also from New Age shops – but it can also be any kind of improvised yard sale junk that you transform and give new life. It depends on you, what you are attracted to and what speaks to you. My first chalice was from a second-hand shop and cost me pennies, but to me it was incredibly beautiful and I was instantly drawn to it. I bought it, cleansed it, charged it and placed it on my little home-made altar. The most important thing is that the tools you gather feel right to you and inspire you in your magick.

Whether you have made or bought your tools, you should cleanse, consecrate and charge them. This should be done with new gemstones, too.

Cleansing Tools and Gemstones

If you have a new tool, cleansing it will remove all previous vibrations. Items pick up the energy of their surroundings, and in order to work effectively with your tools, you want them to be a blank slate that you can then charge and consecrate before you use them in your magick.

There are many ways to cleanse your tools. Here are some of the most common methods:

~ Burn **incense** – preferably sage, which is a popular cleansing agent – over, under and around the object. Feel the smoke cleansing the tool, carrying away any extraneous vibrations with the smoke.

~ **Salt** has been used in many different faiths and cultures to cleanse objects. People tend to prefer sea salt, because it's in a purer form, but any kind of salt will do the trick. Place the object in salt or salt water and leave for a while – or even better, take it for a bath in the ocean. (Don't use this method on items that can be eroded by salt.)

~ **Moonlight** is said to have cleansing properties. During a full moon, put your tools in a place where they will receive direct moonlight and leave them there overnight. Moonlight will not only cleanse but also charge your object with its pure energy.

~ Tools can be cleansed by placing them on a large **amethyst** cluster. Amethyst has a very high spiritual energy and easily absorbs and transforms negative energy (don't forget to cleanse the amethyst cluster in salt water from time to time).

~ **Orgonite** is a device which balances disharmonious energy. Placing your tool on top of a piece of orgonite will remove any excess energy from it – there are orgonite charging plates for this particular purpose, but any piece of orgonite will do. You can read more about orgonite further down in this chapter.

~ To cleanse your object with **sound**, you can (for example) ring a bell around your tool and feel the sound vibrations penetrate and purify it. I once visited a shaman who used a rattle in this same manner.

Consecrating Your Tools

The purpose of consecrating a tool is to bind it to you and make it sacred. After cleansing, your tool is an energetic clean slate. When consecrating your tool, you imbue it with your energy and dedicate it to its specific Divine purpose. This can be done by all sorts of prayers, rituals and meditations.

Here is one suggested ritual which calls on the elements. By way of example I've used a wand, but this ritual can be used for any magickal tool.

Consecration Ritual

Cast your circle.

Turn to the north, hold out your wand and say:

"Guardians of the North, Spirits of Earth
I invite you to consecrate this wand
May it be my sacred and loyal tool in magick
Thank you"

Bow to the Guardians of the North to show your thanks and respect. Now turn to the east, hold out your wand and say:

"Guardians of the East, Spirits of Air
I invite you to consecrate this wand
May it be my sacred and loyal tool in magick
Thank you"

Bow in thanks. Turn to the south, hold out your wand and say:

"Guardians of the South, Spirits of Fire
I invite you to consecrate this wand
May it be my sacred and loyal tool in magick
Thank you"

Bow in thanks. Turn to the west, hold out your wand and say:

"Guardians of the North, Spirits of Earth
I invite you to consecrate this wand
May it be my sacred and loyal tool in magick
Thank you"

Now point your wand to the heavens and say:

"My wand has been consecrated for magickal purposes
May it be blessed by the Goddess and God
Thank you – so mote it be"

This ritual can also be done using various elemental representations:

Earth – sprinkle your tool in soil or sea salt.
Air – hold your tool in incense smoke.
Fire – hold your tool above the flame of a white candle.
Water – sprinkle the tool in water.

Charging Your Tools

The purpose of charging tools is to imbue them with energy. You can imbue them with positive, healing energy or with a specific energy that will aid you in their use. There are a few ways to charge tools:

~ Leaving them in sunlight
~ Praying or chanting
~ Using crystals
~ Using special essential oils that carry high vibrations

My preferred method, however, is to use my holiest, most powerful tool – myself. First, relax into a meditative state. Let your mind run but don't run with it; let all your thoughts flow without paying attention to them, while you concentrate on your breathing. Remain fully in your body.

Now, visualise your head opening up like a funnel, ready to receive pure, divine light. As you breathe in, feel yourself pulling in this bright, warm light through the top of your head down into your body, filling your entire being. Now use your out-breath to direct this light into your tool. Continue doing this and you will feel the tool come alive in your hands, its energy field vibrating in resonance with yours. Keep doing this for as long as you want, whilst focusing on what you intend on using the tool for and what you hope it will do for you.

The DIY Altar

A Wiccan's altar is our holy space, a place dedicated solely to our magick. It is where we keep our tools and our spells, our herbs and crystals; anything that is related to our religion and practice. We are free to decorate it however we want, and it is worth it to go that extra length to make it feel like it represents you. The colour scheme, the fabrics, the decorations, it's all up to you to make it your special, spectacular space.

I adore nature and all things natural, so I like to cover my altar in a myriad of treasures from the woods – stones, feathers, herbs and plants, twigs, dried flowers, anything I find which speaks to me and resonates with who I am. You can put up photos, pieces of fabric, jewellery, items that are holy to you, literally anything. It's a wonderful thing to decorate your altar. (People also like to decorate their altars according to the seasons, and the eight sabbats all have different "altar looks" to accompany them.)

Some might never get round to creating their own altar because they think it has to be costly, but it doesn't have to be. If your budget is a bit tight, or if you don't have much space, here are some ideas for budget household options that might inspire you to create your own do-it-yourself altar.

Altar

For the actual altar you can use anything that will serve as a space to place your magickal items, for example:

~ Any regular desk or table will serve the purpose.

~ A wine crate turned upside down makes a great little sitting altar – and you can store your tools inside it.

~ For an outdoor altar, if you find a wooden board you can place it on rocks, bricks, or tree stumps.

~ Using nature's own resources is very rewarding. Simply place your tools and other items directly onto on a tree stump, a bit of flat rock, or on the ground.

Pentacle

The pentacle is a large flat disc which is inscribed with a magickal symbol, most commonly a pentagram.

The pentagram is a five-sided star which has been used as a spiritual symbol for thousands of years. In ancient Greece, it was thought to represent the five corners in which the seeds of the Universe were planted. In Wicca today, we recognise the pentagram as a representation of the five elements, and the unity of spirit and matter. It is also a powerful symbol of protection.

When the pentacle is used in rituals and spells, it represents a connection to the spiritual world. Often, magickal acts are performed on top of the pentacle, such as consecrating items, gathering herbs together, charging talismans and inscribing or lighting candles.

You can create a pentacle from paper – hand-drawn or a print-out – but if you want a solid pentacle for placing items on, you can:

~ Carve it out of a piece of wood. A slice of a fallen tree with the bark still around it makes for a beautiful earth witch pentacle.

~ Use glass or porcelain paint on a plate, designing your pentacle however you want it – that way you'll have a candle-safe surface, too!

Athame

The athame is a blade that is used to direct energy. Traditionally, the athame is a black-handled knife (since black allows energy to flow through it unhindered) with a double-edged blade, often made of iron. Since a knife is a phallic symbol, the athame represents God energy. As I mentioned in Chapter 1, God energy is forceful, direct and expansive.

The athame represents the element of fire.

An athame can be used to focus and direct energy when casting a circle, consecrating tools, and casting various spells. It can also be used to sever energy ties, as is done in banishing spells.

Because it is used to direct energy, the athame is traditionally straight and symmetrical. For a DIY athame, you can try the following and see which suits you best:

~ Letter openers, preferably straight and double-edged.

~ Metal is a powerful energy transmitter, so a piece of thick metal wire would do the trick.

~ A standard metal nail file can also be used for this purpose.

~ Some witches like to simply extend their arm and direct the energy through it.

Boline

The boline is also a knife, but it is used for physical cutting. The typical boline has a white handle to deflect negativity and intrusive energy, and sometimes has a curved blade like a small scythe.

It is used for purposes such as cutting herbs and inscribing candles. You could use your regular kitchen knife for this, but most witches prefer to have a dedicated tool which is specially consecrated for this task. Even before you have cast the circle you are preparing for the spell, stirring up the energies that you will be transforming. Preparing your spell with a dedicated tool will help set the tone for your spell.

~ You can use any knife with a white handle for this purpose – look in kitchenware or second hand stores. If you want to make it extra special for your ritual purposes, you can decorate it by gluing small crystals onto it, wrapping beads around it, or carving runes or other symbols into it.

Wand

A wand has similar functions to the athame, although there are subtle distinctions. Like the athame, the wand is used to direct energy. It is also a phallic symbol, representative of God energy. However, while athames represent fire, wands represent air.

You may use the wand and athame interchangeably, or just choose one of them to work with. Some witches use athames to direct personal energies, since they correspond with fire and thus with personal will, while they use wands to connect with energies outside the self, as with invocations. As you work with the elements, you should start to feel which energies will be appropriate for the spell you are casting.

~ You can use fallen branch (or you may cut it off a tree, provided you ask the tree for permission first; and it is traditionally expected to offer a small gift in return, such as a gemstone). Go search in nature and pick one that you feel drawn to. You can either leave the bark on if you prefer a more earthy wand with a natural feel, or you can peel of the bark and carve patterns in it, wrap it in coloured string or ribbon, glue beads and crystals to it – let your imagination run wild.

~ For a quick and simple solution – use a chopstick! If you want to decorate it, again you can wrap string or ribbon around it, and to give it a certain energy purpose or boost, glue a small crystal to its tip.

Chalice

The chalice is a vessel that represents the Goddess, feminine energy and the element of water. In the old days, horns and gourds were used for holding liquids during rituals. These days, chalices come in many shapes, sizes and materials. Chalices made out of silver or silver-coloured material are especially widely used, as silver represents the Goddess and the moon.

The chalice is used for holding sacred ritual drinks and for making offerings to the Goddess and God. It can also be used for mixing potions, or to contain salt water that you use to cleanse objects. The chalice is the symbol of the sacred containment of the womb.

~ Sometimes in flea markets you can find old copper chalices, but if you're not that lucky, just use a wine glass. You can use some glass paint to decorate it, perhaps with a pentagram.

Cauldron

The cauldron, like the chalice, also corresponds with Goddess energy and the womb. Traditionally, the cauldron is made of brass and has three legs which represent the Maiden, the Mother and the Crone, the three aspects of the Goddess. The cauldron corresponds with water, but also with fire. It represents transmutation and change.

The cauldron may also be used to contain sacred liquids, or to make brews or potions. It also makes a safe container for burning items. The cauldron can also be used for scrying when filled with water.

~ If you plan on using your cauldron for brewing herbs and potions, then you can use a cast iron pot (or any saucepan) in your kitchen. If, however, you want a cauldron mainly for a ritual bowl or a fireproof dish, then any porcelain kitchen bowl, metal bowl, or even ashtray will work fine.

Broom

The witch's broom is also known as the besom. It usually has a wooden handle, and is traditionally made up of ash, birch and willow.

The broom is used for sweeping away negative or unwanted energies, and for clearly defining a space of magickal work. Use the broom to sweep an area before casting a circle, doing so in clockwise motions.

According to folklore, the broom protects negative energies from entering when it is placed across a threshold such as a doorway.

~ It is always fun to make a traditional homemade broom, using a thick branch or stick for a handle and thin branches such as birch tree ends wrapped and wound around it.

~ Any regular broom or sweep will do the trick.

~ Cleaning dusters are very satisfying for sweeping the air clean of energies.

~ Go out into nature and find some feathers, and tie them together for a great energy sweep.

The Goddess and God

Some witches like to have representations of the Goddess and God (or other deities they may worship) on their altar. Here are some examples of what to use for this purpose.

~ A common one is to have two candles – silver for the Goddess and gold for the God.

~ Little figurines or small statues you may come across that you feel represent the deities. You can also make your own figurines out of clay or Fimo, or natural craft materials such as rocks, twigs and pinecones.

~ You can use artwork and place it on or above your altar, perhaps framed. Make your own or print pictures from the internet.

Offering dish

An offering dish can be used to hold various things that you would like to offer to the Goddess and God, various entities and other spirits. When it comes to making an offering, you are not offering up the physical item but rather the energetic representation of it, so choose things that are meaningful to you – perhaps flowers which you think are beautiful, your favourite fruit, even a piece of jewellery that is special to you.

~ Use any dish or plate – you may find a beautiful one in a flea market or yard sale, or look in your grandmother's attic for old china she no longer uses. It is also rewarding to buy a plain plate or bowl and decorate it yourself with glass paints.

Using Crystals in Magick

Crystals have been thought of as magickal objects in many different cultures throughout the ages. Aside from their fetching beauty, their symmetrical inner structure, formed under extreme pressures and temperatures, makes them incredibly dense and focused. They have their own energy field, which we utilise in magick and healing. Some people think that they are etheric templates which contain a blueprint for healing, harmonious energy.

They have a higher consciousness and respond well to our intent, meaning they absorb the energies we direct to them. Programmed crystals are able to hold vast amounts of information, which is why they work so well in magick. Once you have charged the crystal with your intention, it will remember this and carry on emitting and attracting those energies after the spell is cast.

Crystals for healing

Crystals emanate balanced, harmonious frequencies, and by having them around us and tuning in to them, our body's own natural energy begins to entrain to their harmonising energies. For example, rose quartz emits the frequency of love and nurturing, so whenever you have rose quartz near you, your energy body will attune to its loving frequency.

Place a crystal over a part of your body that is in need of healing. Do this regularly and healing will speed up, since the symmetrical, orderly structure of the crystal will work to restore balance and stabilise the energies around it.

As with most things, the amount of healing depends on how much you are opening yourself up to the crystal's energy. By connecting with the crystal several times daily, you increase your channels to receive that crystal's specific vibration. You should also cleanse, charge and consecrate your crystals when you first obtain them, in order to get the best effects.

You can meditate with your crystals, while holding them in your hand or placing them near you during the meditation. This will help focus your mind and restore balance in your energy field, and will also increase your connection with your Higher Self.

Crystals and their properties

Crystals carry different purposes and vibrations, so you will want to make sure that you choose the appropriate stones for your desired outcome. Below is a list of some of the most common crystals and their properties. If you want to dig deeper, there is plenty of information online as well as a vast array of helpful books on the subject.

Amber	Cleansing; brings positive energy, strength and confidence.
Amethyst	Spiritual wisdom and connection; protects against and transforms negativity.
Angelite	Connects you to your angels and guides; promotes inner peace and guidance.
Aquamarine	Aids in letting go of negative emotions and fosters inner tranquillity.
Black Tourmaline	Grounding and powerful protection; repels negative energy.
Bloodstone	Instils courage, strength and endurance through adversity.
Carnelian	Awakens vitality, courage, focus, and passion.
Citrine	Enhances creativity, confidence and abundance.
Clear Quartz	Amplifies all energy and intent; brings purification, clarity and balance.
Emerald	Brings intuition, wisdom and healing of the heart.
Fluorite	Heals the aura; assists in meditation and allows for higher levels of intuition.
Garnet	Increases self-esteem and interpersonal relationships; soothes anger.
Hematite	Protective and grounding; brings integration and balance in all areas.
Jade	Promotes luck, abundance and positive growth.
Labradorite	Protects from negativity; useful for earth magick and visualisation.

Lapis Lazuli	The Truth Stone; enhances spiritual clarity and self-awareness.
Peridot	A powerful cleanser; releases physical toxins and negative emotions.
Red Jasper	Strengthens the physical body; balances sexuality and protects against negativity.
Rose Quartz	Attracts love and friendship; a nurturing and soothing heart healer.
Ruby	Promotes abundance, passion, joy and success.
Smoky Quartz	Grounds and protects against negativity.
Sugilite	Aids spiritual connection, universal love, understanding and awareness.
Sunstone	A joyful stone which promotes optimism, courage and good fortune.
Tiger's Eye	Attracts prosperity and personal success; powerfully protective and calming.
Turquoise	A master healer which brings inner calm and deep healing.

Orgonite – the crystal amplifier

Orgonite is another tool which is only now starting to become recognised in the Wiccan community. It is based on the findings of Austrian Dr Reich, who was one of the few scientists to ever have studied life-force energy, or what he called "orgone".

He observed small particles of life-energy and how they interacted with physical matter. By doing this, he was able to construct an orgone accumulator, a device made of metals and carbon-based substances which drew energy inside it. A person who was ill would sit inside the device, and Reich would see improvements in their health.

Orgonite is made from metals, resins and crystals. It works in a similar way to crystals, by emitting a healing, balancing frequency. Orgonite is constantly drawing in stagnant energy and emitting clean, fresh energy, and has a wider range of effectiveness than most crystals. In complement to the other crystals and gemstones it contains (to create various properties and purposes), there is also a quartz crystal which is put under pressure by the cured resin, creating a tiny electrical spark that magnifies its healing effect.

Using Candles in Magick

Candle magick is a very common form of magick, which utilises the element of fire (to initiate change or transform or release something which is no longer wanted) and the properties and purposes of the different colours. This type of magick particularly relies on the power of visualisation and intent.

Look at the colour chart below and figure out which candle would be most appropriate for your purpose. Before the ritual or spellcasting, prepare the candle by consecrating or charging it. To consecrate it, dip your finger in oil (you can buy special anointing oil from New Age shops, or you can use olive oil) and run it up and down the candle a couple of times, while directing your intent into the candle. Ask of it to help you accomplish your goal. To charge it, hold it in your hands and feel your energies merging with it, pulling up the energies of the candle each time you breathe in, and filling the candle with your own energies as you breathe out.

You can also carve symbols, runes, initials and more into the candle – things that represent the result you wish to achieve.

Candle colours and their properties

White contains all colours. It symbolises purity and innocence, and the Maiden aspect of the Triple Goddess. Use for purification, peace, healing, truth and sincerity, cleansing, spirituality, clarity, wholeness and joy. It can also protect, repel negative energy, relieve tension and aid in meditation.

Yellow is the realm of intellect, inspiration and creativity. Use for confidence and charm, persuasion, wisdom, mental strength, concentration, communication, memory, logic and learning. It stimulates your personal power and self-esteem, and promotes cheerfulness and an optimistic outlook. Use it to invoke or represent the element of Air.

Orange is energising and promotes stimulation, joy and success. Use for good fortune, prosperity, power, action, energy building, and courage. Aids in legal matters, achieving goals, cleansing negative attitudes and bringing in happiness and enthusiasm. Also used for attracting friends and inspires emotional healing.

Pink represents all variations of love – friendly, romantic, spiritual, and universal. Use for love magick, compassion, forgiveness, joy, harmony, sensitivity, emotional and spiritual healing, and self-love. Promotes spiritual awakening and opening of the heart.

Red is the colour of fire and passion. It represents activity and action, blood, love, sex, fertility, potency, power, vitality, and courage. It instils energy and strength and can thus be used for health, vigour and defence. It also symbolises the Mother aspect of the Triple Goddess. Use it to invoke or represent the element of Fire.

Purple is a highly spiritual colour and is associated with psychic abilities, spiritual awakening, and ancient wisdom. It is the colour of the third eye chakra where your psychic vision and inner eye reside, so purple can be used to open your third eye in order to invite visions and enhance intuition. Use also for spiritual protection, healing, respect, honour, wisdom, purification, sensitivity, progress, spiritual growth and dissociating from the ego. Meditate regularly with a purple candle to reduce stress or insomnia.

Magenta is used to facilitate quick changes and fast results in spell work. Burn with another candle to increase the energy of that candle's purpose and intent. Also used for exorcism and spiritual healing.

Blue is a soothing colour and is connected to spirituality, inner peace, and harmony. Promotes wisdom, truth, tranquillity, rest, healing, serenity, patience and kindness. Burned for dream magick and prophetic dreams. Encourages loyalty, understanding, and a peaceful home. Use it to invoke or represent the element of Water. Meditate with a blue candle to help focus your mind.

Turquoise is used for stress relief, focus and intellect. Aids in storing knowledge, improving memory, and finding logic in any situation.

Green is associated with nature, growth, and fertility, and is a symbol of the Goddess and her green earth. It is also a colour often linked to money and financial success. Use for luck and prosperity, abundance and generosity, earth magick, physical and emotional healing, rejuvenation, and renewal. Assists agriculture to encourage a good harvest. Use it to invoke or represent the element of Earth.

Brown is the colour of earth, and holds a grounded, balanced vibration. Assists in clear thinking and decision-making. Promotes concentration, intuition, material gain, wealth, common sense, and stability. Also encourages intuition and telepathic abilities. It is said to help locate lost objects. Also used to protect and heal animals.

Silver (or grey) is a neutral colour and can be used to deflect and neutralise negative influences. It brings protection against otherworldly entities, stabilises energies, and promotes inner peace and serenity. Also a symbol of the Goddess, and can be used to invoke any female deity.

Gold is associated with the God and solar deities. It is believed to attract the powers of cosmic influences. Encourages success, wealth, communication, persuasion, victory, masculine energy, and confidence. Use when invoking any male deity.

Black absorbs all colours, and is often used to absorb or banish negativity. It reverses curses and hexes. Use for protection, banishing, repelling black magick, and ridding of bad habits. It enhances inner strength, resilience and self-control, and can be used in meditation to delve deeper into the unconscious. Also burned for powerful healing and support through loss and grief. Represents the Crone aspect of the Triple Goddess.

Using Herbs in Magick

Way before history books and Western medicine, herbs were used for various remedies and medications, brewed into potions, kept in amulets and talismans, and burned as incense to keep evil at bay. Herbs that held a high vibration would be used for protection since they could ward off negative influences, and thus were often hung in doorways and around houses, burned, or otherwise kept nearby.

Herbal magick works in a similar way to crystal and candle magick, in that it utilises the inherent properties of the herbs in combination with the focus and intent of the witch. As you prepare your herbs, focus on your intentions for your brew, incense or potion in order to infuse the herbs with your energies, thus increasing their potency and directing them towards your desired outcome.

The herbs, like the crystals, have a consciousness of their own, and showing respect and gratitude for their work will increase their effectiveness even further. Wherever you can, use home-grown, wild-picked, or organic plants. If you are growing your own, make sure you consecrate the tools you will be using – for example, boline for harvesting and cutting, mortar and pestle for crushing and grinding. You may also want to keep a mug or other container which is especially intended for your brews.

Mother Earth has kindly provided us with plants for any kind of physical ailment and magickal intention, and you will find plenty of information in books and online that will help you choose your herbs. If you plan on mixing different herbs, remember that often less is more – if you put too many varieties into the mix you may end up diluting their strengths and properties. Also note that some herbs are toxic and not for human ingestion – always make sure you are safe.

If you want to get started with herbology, find a book that speaks to you and get studying – there is a lot of information to absorb! Before long you will be able to make your own brews and potions, talismans and charm bags, potpourris and incenses, and maybe even more complex things like oils and lotions. If you have the option, you may want to start growing your own herbs. It is a joy to bring these little gems up from tiny seeds into full-grown plants, and then to be able to enjoy their gifts.

These are some of the most common herbs and their corresponding properties:

Angelica Root	Protects against negative energy; heals and clears the aura.
Basil	Used for love and prosperity spells; brings luck and purification.
Bay leaves	Enhances intuition and psychic abilities; also useful for protection and purification.
Chamomile	Attracts love and prosperity; chamomile tea is a relaxant often used for meditation or sleep.
Cinnamon	Brings success and abundance; can also be used to increase spirituality.
Garlic	Used for protection, healing and purification spells.
Lavender	Brings love, peace and happiness.
Mugwort	Enhances divination and brings prophetic dreams.
Patchouli	Associated with wealth, love and lust; can also be used as a fertility talisman.
Rosemary	Used for purification and cleansing, and healing of all kinds.
Sage	Highly purifying and cleansing; enhances wisdom and longevity.
Thyme	Cleanses old vibrations; also used to promote good health.
Yarrow	Brings courage, self-esteem and love; dispels negative energy and melancholia.

CHAPTER 6

Living in tune with your body

In order to achieve the best possible results in your magick, you must be able to work with your most precious tool – your body. When you are living in harmony with your body, energy flows unobstructed through you which leads to balance, health, and clarity. These are all important factors in successful magick.

Many of us take our bodies for granted, and mistreat or even abuse them through stress, excessive exercise or none at all, unhealthy eating, low self-esteem, and so on. Wiccans know that our bodies are holy temples, temporarily lent to us so that we may experience this gift of life.

Unfortunately it is also common to dislike the way our bodies look – no wonder, due to the pressures of society and media. But no matter your physical appearance, your body is the most magnificent machine known to man; a wonderful combination of cells that make up this temporary home of yours, which allows you to experience the world through your senses.

In order to live in tune with your body you must learn to listen to it. It is far more intelligent than your mind and it knows what it needs – when something is missing, it will tell you. Pay attention to the signs from your body and try your best to feed it nutritious and varied foods, drink enough water and try to get outside for some exercise, fresh air and connection with nature as often as you can.

Honour and love your body, and know that it is working hard day and night to keep you alive. Your body has a consciousness of its own, and by appreciating and loving it you are helping and healing it. Use the exercises below to release any obstructing negative emotions you may be carrying around, to reinstate free flow and balance in your body.

Finally, remember to enjoy and appreciate your body while you have it. Sing, laugh, dance, and eat good foods whenever you can. Every day is a precious gift and by enjoying your life you honour and thank the Goddess and God for bringing you on this adventure.

(To say daily thanks to your body, see the *Body Appreciation Prayer* under Spells and Rituals.)

Recognising and releasing emotions

One of the most powerful skills we can have as witches is the ability to listen to our emotions. Emotions are one of our main ways of receiving information about the non-physical world of energy. In fact, emotions *are* energy.

Powerful emotions manifest as physical sensations in our body. Negative (low-frequency) emotions may manifest as sharp, heavy, or painful sensations, while positive (high-frequency) emotions can manifest as light, airy, energising, and sometimes bubbly sensations. Your true essence – your Higher Self – is made up of free-flowing, high-frequency energy, and low-frequency energy thus disrupts the flow and can result in pain.

It is important to note, however, that negative emotions are not inherently bad. Rather, they are powerful indicators that you are somehow off your path, straying too far from your Higher Self – that is why it is vital that we learn to listen to them without judging them, in order to follow their loving guidance. Energy wants to flow freely through you – a process that happens when you allow the energy to be, without avoidance or judgement.

It can be tempting to suppress negative emotions or distract ourselves in order to not have to deal with them, but in the long run we are only causing ourselves more damage. The act of suppressing is very unhealthy since we are denying our emotions – meeting them with resistance, thus creating a blockage in our energy field. The energy just wants to flow through you by being acknowledged and felt, but the resistance blocks it so that it can't go anywhere. It's like pinching the end of a hose that has water flowing through it – in lack of an exit way, pressure builds up and results in pain.

This resistance is often an energy blockage brought on by beliefs which you have formed throughout your life, many of them in childhood. These beliefs may be subtle or even subconscious, but they result in feeling cut off from your Higher Self. The resistance can also be an energy blockage brought on by the fact that you are on a path that isn't aligned with your Higher Self.

As you progress with your training as a Wiccan, you will begin to connect more to your Higher Self, especially if you practice the many spiritual exercises provided in this book. As this happens, many of these energy blockages will dissipate on their own.

For more stubborn emotions, however, the following exercise will help. While performing it, it's important to have an attitude of non-judgement and acceptance. Remember that negative emotions are in no way harmful if you only allow yourself to feel them. Recognise them as messengers from your Higher Self, telling you that you are somehow disconnected from your path.

Exercise:

Connect to the Goddess and God. Feel their infinite love and wisdom as a glowing light emanating from all directions, being pulled towards your heart area.

Now think of the negative emotion that you have, and place your focus inside your body. How does the energy of the emotion feel? Try to feel it as a sensation – is it hot, cold, prickly? Avoid giving it names such as anger, hate or fear. For now, we are just concerned with the physical sensation of the emotion. For a few moments, try to get a sense of this feeling, without judging it. By focusing on the physical sensation you are acknowledging and feeling the emotion, which is a first and major step towards releasing it.

For each sensation you identify, focus on it, notice how it feels, and say:

"Through the abundant love of the Goddess and God, I accept this feeling as a perfect part of the Universe. It's only temporary, and it serves to teach me something."

Imagine a gentle, soft beam of light emanating from your heart and shining onto the area. Simply beam that light onto it while feeling supported by the love and light of the Goddess and God. As you do so, you might find that the feeling changes shape, size or location. Just continue emanating acceptance and love onto whatever sensation you feel, for as long as you feel it.

What you are doing is softening the blockage by connecting it with the love emanating from the Goddess and God and your Higher Self. By bathing it in love and acceptance, the energy will begin to flow more freely, which will help it release. Eventually it will begin to leave your energy field, and you will notice that the feeling diminishes or disappears.

If you want to give this exercise a boost, hold a piece of rose quartz while performing it.

Clearing your aura

Since your energy plays such a major role in your magick, having a clear energy field is essential if you want to achieve the best possible results. All that you encounter in your life will leave a mark on your aura, and it's up to you whether you choose to let it go or allow it to stay. As they say, 'You can't stop a bird from landing on your head, but you can stop it from building a nest.'

We all carry things we would do best to get rid of. Here is an exercise for letting go of unwanted energies and releasing negative baggage in order to become clear and focused. This can be done whenever you want, but if you're feeling mentally or emotionally muddled before casting a spell, that would be a particularly good time for this exercise.

Perform this ritual somewhere where the energy you release has an exit way – I recommend that you do it by an open window through which you can release any energies and entities from your field. In this case you will direct the energy out through the window and return to the light or "other side" (wherever it can go to be at peace). Another good place for this exercise is the shower, where you can make use of the running water washing you clean. You would then visualise the energy releasing with the water and flowing safely into the ground.

Stand, relax your shoulders, release your neck. Feel your feet against the floor. Take some deep breaths. Make the out-breaths as long and slow as you comfortably can, since this produces relaxation hormones in your body and will relax your entire energy field – an essential starting place for releasing energy.

You will now address the energies you are about to release, in a firm but loving manner – the way a parent might speak to their child. Talk to the energies or entities along the lines of the suggested incantation below, repeating the words over and over. Find words to this effect that you feel comfortable with.

"Any energy that no longer serves me, please leave now.
Thank you for your presence, now please go. I am sending you home.
Go back whence you came; go into the light, where you will be at peace.
You have served your purpose, now I am releasing you.
I am sending you home. Please leave NOW. Please leave NOW."

Really *feel* every word and their impact as you speak. Look out for sensations in your body, like a lifting or pulling sensation, or a change in temperature. Repeat the words until you feel some sort of release or final tug, or you just sense that you are finished. There is no telling how long it will take – it could be anything from a brief minute to several repeated attempts. You should know, though, that the sooner you *believe* it can be released, the sooner it will *be* released.

When I was younger and first learning about energy, I used this method to release an entity which had attached itself to my lower back. I had had intense cramps in my lower abdomen, but was unaware of the fact that an otherworldly entity that had taken up residence near my tailbone, until I met with two spiritual healers who could both see it. They said it was of a mellow grey colour, which suggests a low-frequency being, but it wasn't terribly ill-meaning or it would have been darker or even black.

We stood by the window and I began chanting words along the lines of the ones above. My healers told me they couldn't do it for me – they could promote a peaceful parting by holding a high energy and helping me through it, but I had to be the one doing the talking, since I was the one releasing the entity from my energy field.

After saying the words a few times I began feeling a pulling sensation around my hips, like it was slowly leaving my field and drawing towards the window. It was the strangest feeling! Within minutes, suddenly both healers drew their breath and said it was gone. One of them was kinaesthetic and had felt the being leave peacefully, and the other was clairvoyant and had seen it leave my aura and bow slightly to thank me for having released it. As ever with magick, I was truly amazed. What's more, my abdominal cramps went away, never to return.

Afterwards, I was told of the importance to fill the new gaps in my energy field where the entity had resided. You do this by imagining the top of your head opening up into a funnel, sucking down divine and healing light. Say out loud:

"I ask that pure and healing light enter my body
And fill my entire being with bright, white light
Pure, healing, divine light
Thank you"

Draw down the healing light as you breathe in, and visualise it filling every nook and cranny in and around your energy field. Do this actively for a few minutes, and then occasionally throughout the day, take a couple of deep breaths to recharge the flow of divine light.

The seven major chakras

Throughout this book I mention the body's *chakras*, or energy centers. The image below shows you where these chakras are located, and the table tells you the purposes and properties of each one:

THE SEVEN CHAKRAS

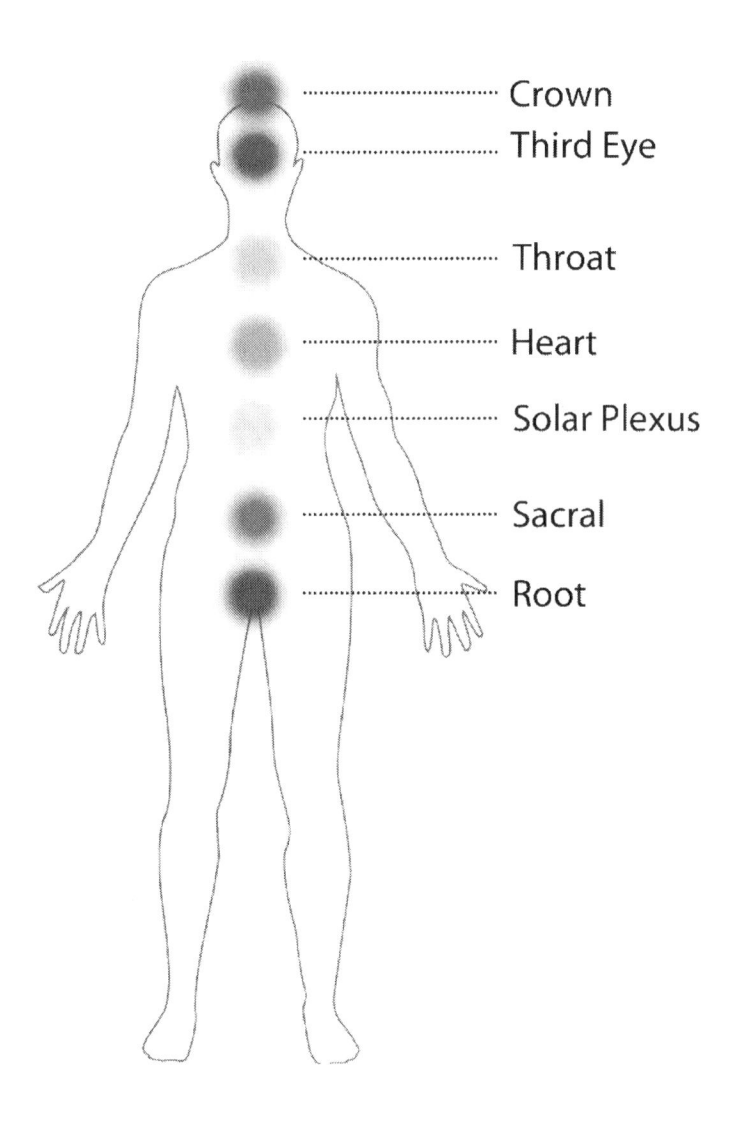

- Crown
- Third Eye
- Throat
- Heart
- Solar Plexus
- Sacral
- Root

Crown
(Violet)
This chakra connects us to our Higher Selves and to the Universe. We receive guidance and higher wisdom through our crown chakra, and it allows us to feel a true spiritual connection to everything that exists.

Third Eye
(Indigo)
This is the chakra of insight, where we connect with our spirituality and intuition. The third eye chakra connects us to our inner wisdom, allowing us to think clearly and see the bigger picture.

Throat
(Blue)
This is the center of communication and self-expression. The throat chakra helps us to express our authentic selves and speak our truth to the world with confidence.

Heart
(Green)
This chakra is related to love, understanding, and universal interconnectedness. It allows us to feel compassion and a deep connection to everyone around us, as well as a loving relationship with ourselves.

Solar
Plexus
(Yellow)
Often called the power chakra, this is our seat of personal power. It governs our self-respect, balance and discipline.

Sacral
(Orange)
This is our center of emotions, creativity, and sensuality. A healthy sacral chakra promotes intuition, self-worth, and healthy relationships with others.

Root
(Red)
This is the survival chakra which connects us to the physical world. It also governs our base sexuality. The root chakra grounds us and gives us a sense of belonging and stability.

(Please note that when carrying out chakra work, it is highly recommended to start with the Root, which is the first chakra, and work our way up.)

SPELLS AND RITUALS

Crafting spells

In the previous chapters of this book you will have found plenty of information that will help you craft your own spells, such as what deities to invoke, what crystals to use, and how to focus your energy. In this section of the book you will find a wide range of example spells to show this information being put into practice. Practice whichever ones you feel drawn to, re-write them to suit your purposes, or use them as inspiration to write your own spells. Each spell is clearly worded and is accompanied by a breakdown of the ingredients and their properties, so that you can see why I have chosen those specific tools and components.

To help further your understanding of spellcrafting, here is a breakdown of the crafting process that will help you write your own successful spells.

The crafting process – a step-by-step guide

Step 1: The purpose of the spell

Figure out what you want. The Universe can bring you anything you desire, but you must *know what you want*. If you send out confused, uncertain, or otherwise muddled energies, then what you receive back won't be of much substance. Likewise, if you carry on focusing on the problem (e.g. *"I don't have enough money"* or *"I am too fat"*) then you are still not focusing on what you *want*. You are focusing on what you *don't* want. Keep doing that and the Universe will bring you more of the same. Remember, *"What ye send forth comes back to thee, so ever mind the Law of Three."* Decide on what you are asking for, and make that the angle of the spell.

Step 2: Suitable ingredients

Consider what tools and ingredients could be useful for your purpose. Is it love-related? Look to the colours pink and red; use rose quartz; invoke deities who are in charge of the love realm, for example Eros, Cupid,

Venus and Freya; use herbs such as lavender, yarrow, patchouli and basil. Is it for money? Use coins or gold in your spell, the colour green, crystals such as green aventurine and peridot, and call upon Lakshmi or Moneta to assist you. Read other spell books or go online and see how similar spells have been constructed in the past. Jot down some notes and build up the skeleton of your spell.

Step 3: Break it down

Now that you have your purpose and your ingredients, construct it into sections. If I want to cast a love spell, for example, I might break it down into something like this:

1. Addressing the Spirits/Elements/Deities etc, asking for their presence and assistance.
2. Healing old hurt to make way for new love.
3. Visualising the perfect person coming into my life and sending out energies to attract this someone.
4. Calling the person to me and sealing the spell.

Once you have an outline that you are happy with, move to the final step – writing your spell.

Step 4: The writing

Now put it all in order. What do you want to do first? When do you light the candle(s) and incense? Will you charge something, or maybe create a talisman? What type of visualisation work is required? Do you want to invoke any entities to assist you? Use your imagination here to put the final spell together – add anything that you feel would aid your spell; any incantation that feels appropriate. Address any spirit or deity you wish. Double-check that any candles, herbs and crystals are in accordance with your desired outcome.

There you have it! Now, you just need to find time and space to do the casting. How exciting! It's a good idea to keep a magick journal (unless you have a Book of Shadows, in which case you could keep a journal in there) where you keep notes of how you felt during the casting, if you experienced any particular sensations, and what happened afterwards and how soon you began to feel changes and see results. Perhaps there was something that didn't feel right which you would like to change for your next spell. This is a great tracker for your future spell work.

The weight of words

Before we learn language, our thoughts exist in abstract and conceptual form. We then grow older and learn to communicate through words, and begin to think and speak in concrete terms. Our thoughts become words, and these words have tremendous power.

We use words all the time, to communicate our thoughts and ideas to others and respond to theirs, as well as in our constant dialogue with ourselves and the Universe. Words carry certain vibrations, associations and understandings, and it's important to realise the weight of these words and their impact on our lives.

Using words in magick

Words play a great role in spellcasting. We express our desires through incantations, communicating with the Spirits, the Goddess and God, and our own guardian angels and guides. The Universe hears our prayers. Therefore it is vital that we phrase them correctly.

Let's say we are casting a spell to bring more money into our lives. Consider the difference between the following two phrases:

"I need money to pay my debt; please bring me money so I will no longer be poor."

"I love having money to have fun and be free; please bring me money so that I will live in abundance."

The two phrases express the same desire, and still they are very different. The latter sentence is clearly phrased not to contain any negatively charged words or phrases (or rather, to only contain positively charged words and phrases – see what I mean?), and it carries a much higher vibration.

Since everything we express sparks a reaction on some level of reality, positively phrased, highly charged phrases will create reactions of the same vibration. *"What ye send forth comes back to thee"* – this applies also to your words.

Watch how you express yourself during spellcasting (and in your everyday life), and make sure that you phrase your communications and incantations in a way that will reflect good back to you.

To illustrate the point...

I don't want to be alone – I am looking forward to finding a companion

I need to ease my stress – I love having peace of mind

I don't want to be poor – I am looking forward to wealth and abundance

I need to get rid of my fear – I love feeling confident and at ease

I wish I had something better – I am grateful for what I have, but aim for more

> ***Watch how you are speaking to yourself,***
> ***because you are listening.***

⛤

"For the highest good"

My favourite words in spell work or prayer is this highly significant phrase, *for the highest good*. Adding these words to the end of any incantation will ensure that whatever you wish for will be brought to you insofar as it does not interfere with anybody's free will, nor does it harm anyone in your way. It shows care for the bigger picture and a humility before the workings of the Universe. The Goddess and God will take note of your benevolence and respond accordingly.

LOVE SPELL – PART 1

Spell to Release Pain from Past Loves

We all need love in our lives, but if you have been hurt in the past it can sometimes be difficult to release old negativity in order to make way for new love to enter your life. If you are looking to ease yourself of this pain, and in particular if you want to attract new love into your life, this is an essential step towards both self-healing and finding future relationships.

Cast this spell before casting the Love Spell which comes after this, to ensure that you are in the best possible position to find new love.

What you need:
Sage incense
Pen and paper
1 onion
Boline (if you don't have one, use a regular knife)

Let's begin…

Light the incense.

Use your pen and paper to write about your previous hurts. This is to release all the negative feelings you are currently holding surrounding love and companionship. If you have been feeling lonely or hurt, write it all down now in order to let go of it.

Write without stopping or thinking, just let it flow. This will likely bring up some painful emotions, but that is part of the process. Place all of your hurt onto the paper.

When the words stop flowing, fold the paper and relax for a moment. Breathe deeply to regain your inner balance. When you feel ready, cast your circle.

Take the onion and hold it in your hands. This will absorb the negativity you have released. Use the boline to make a deep cut into the middle of the onion, and then place your paper in it.

"From past pain to future gain
Onion, take my hurt away
From now the pain is kept at bay
Darkness goes and light remains"

Hold the onion with the paper inside it and feel yourself becoming light and relieved. Look within yourself to see if you are holding any remaining negativity. Whatever you find, focus it into the onion.

Close your circle. Bury the onion (with the paper inside it) somewhere safe in the ground. As you cover it with soil, feel your past pains dissipate into Mother Earth. You are free and ready to receive new love and joy.

Spell breakdown

Sage is a powerful cleanser and protector, which also promotes clarity, wisdom, and healing of the spirit. Burn it to purify any space and person within that space.

Onions absorb negativity and can be used to help let go of bad habits and negative energies. As you put the paper inside it, it will soak up the energy you have spilled onto the paper. As you later bury it, you fully let go of this old energy and release it into Mother Earth's healing care.

LOVE SPELL – PART 2

Spell to Attract Love

Before performing this spell, you should have cast the previous spell to release past hurt. This will help clear blockages that you might be holding from past relationships, which may be standing in your way of finding true love.

What you need:
Incense: vanilla or patchouli
1 pink candle
Pen and paper
1 red apple
Boline (if you don't have one, use a regular knife)
1 red ribbon

Let's begin…

Light the incense.

Think of the type of relationship you would like to have. Imagine the feeling of having the perfect companion. How would you like to feel when you're with him or her? How would you like to spend a day together?

Take your pen and paper and write about this imagined, perfect relationship. Write from the heart, freely and joyfully, as if you already had this love in your life. Writing in present tense helps align your energies with the reality of what you desire.

Rather than focusing on specific traits or physical appearance, concentrate on the feelings of the relationship – joy, love, care, loyalty, companionship, a magnetic attraction, passion; whatever you wish for. Write about how you love spending time together, how confident you feel with him or her, how attracted you are to this person, and anything else you wish for in your ideal relationship.

When you feel ready, cast your circle and light the candle.

Sit down and relax for a moment. Now read aloud what you've written on your paper, while you feel yourself becoming joyful and excited. The positive energy of your imagined relationship fills the circle as you speak. Imagine a warm, glowing light emanating from your heart, filling the circle and spilling onto your written words.

Fold up your paper and place it next to the candle. Take the apple and use the boline to cut it in half. Hold one half in each hand and say:

"Two souls, destined to join in love
The perfect union; a gift from above
The linking of hearts now has begun
An apple for love, two halves become one"

Place the paper in between the two halves and tie them together with the ribbon. Hold it in your hands whilst knowing that love will come to you in the perfect time. Feel your gratitude towards the Goddess and God for this future relationship.

Close your circle. Throw the apple in a river or stream.

Spell breakdown

Vanilla incense attracts love and passion, and strengthens the powers of your mind in order to achieve your goals.

Patchouli incense is used in love spells and money spells. Promotes positive growth and new beginnings.

Pink candles encourage healthy relationships and emotional understanding. It is burned to manifest romantic and loyal love.

The heart is the center of your being and is a place of powerful healing, regeneration and manifestation.

The apple is a traditional symbol of love, and is often used in love spells and potions to attract romance.

Water represents emotions and deeper connections.

Goddess Spell for Plant Growth

Cast this spell when you are about to plant something – herbs, trees, houseplants – to call upon the Goddess for her blessing to encourage healthy growth.

What you need:
A green candle
Wooden matches
A glass of water
Your seeds and planting accessories

Let's begin...

Cast a circle. Stand or sit within it and relax. Light the candle with a match, and say:

"Great Mother Goddess, I honour thee
In this ritual for thriving growth, please join me"

Light the green candle with a match and say:

"Element of Earth, I welcome thee."

Dip your hands in the glass of water and say:

"Element of Water, I welcome thee."

With the water on your fingertips, touch the green candle and say:

"Earth and Water, please combine
Creating life for these [plants/herbs/trees] of mine"

Place your seeds before you and raise your arms to the heavens. Say:

"Goddess, lady of fertility and growth
God, spirit of forest and thriving nature
I call upon thee to bless these [plants/herbs/trees]
May they sprout and grow and thrive
Flourishing in your loving gaze

Thank you – so mote it be"
Take the glass of water and hold it in your hands. Close your eyes and visualise your plants growing, wild and strong; think of an old forest, a jungle of thriving growth. Hold on to this image for as long as possible, and feel your hands charging the glass of water with this joyful image and feeling.

When you feel intuitively done, open your eyes and take a deep breath. Now sprinkle the water on top of the soil, and say:

"With blessed and charged water, I bring you to life."

Close your circle. Thank the Goddess, God, Spirits and Elements for their presence and assistance.

You can also connect to the seeds by meditating in front of them. Sit with them until your mind is completely still, and then ask them what they need in order to grow healthy and strong. If your mind is quiet enough, you may receive an answer – it may be an energetic communication from the seeds that is interpreted by your mind, or a message from the spirits letting you know what must be done for your spell to work.

Spell breakdown

Green candles symbolise Mother Earth and the Goddess, and promote fertility, growth and rejuvenation.

Earth represents growth and stability, and we call on it to enhance our connection with nature.

Water is healing and nourishing, and promotes renewal and adaptation to one's surroundings.

Spell to Repair a Relationship or Friendship

Relationships are perhaps the most important part of life – and I mean any relationship we have with any person, not just a lover. Your relationships with family members, friends, co-workers – anyone who is connected to you and influences your life.

We are all individuals and being close to someone usually involves some compromise. We won't always agree with each other, and there may be fallouts.

This spell is to set these relationships and friendships straight, to regain balance between two people, and erase old quarrels.

What you need:
1 pink candle
Incense (preferably Benzoin or Sweet Pea, otherwise Frankincense)
2 pieces of string

Let's begin…

Cast your circle.

Place the two pieces of string on either side of the candle. As you light it, repeat the following words three times:

"Friendship, kindness, understanding, love."

Hold the left piece of string in your hand. Say:

"This string represents me, and all that I am."

Hold the right piece of string in your hand. Say:

"This string represents [Name] and all that [he/she] is."

Place them back on either side of the candle.

Light the incense. As it burns, feel the smoke fill the air and visualise it burning away any negativity or misunderstandings between you. Feel its healing scent patching up old wounds and rekindling your relationship with this person.

Take the two pieces of string and hold them above the candle for a moment. Say:

"Two people of two kinds
Meet and make friends
A union of minds
As Philotes intends"

Now tie the two pieces of string together, as you say the following:

"I ask for reunion as we now intertwine
To see their perspective, and they to see mine
May we gain wisdom to love and set free
With kindness and care; so mote it be"

Close your circle and blow out the candle. Let the incense burn to the end.

Bury the tied-together strings underneath a bush or tree in your garden, or place it in a plant pot somewhere in your house.

When you next see this person, remember the spell and the feelings that came up during your casting. See if you can act differently towards the person – more open, friendly and understanding, and you will see how their behaviour towards you changes, too.

Spell breakdown

Pink candles are burned to nurture relationships, to encourage loyalty and friendship, and promote healing of the spirit.

Benzoin is burned for purification which will help clear any negativity between you. It helps bring emotional balance, and lifts painful emotions such as depression, lethargy, anger, anxiety and grief.

Sweet Pea is burned for friendship and love, and inspires courage.

Frankincense dispels negativity and will also work to clear the baggage between you.

Philotes is the Greek Goddess of friendship and affection.

Beauty Spell

To be perceived as attractive by other people, we must first feel attractive to ourselves. We change within, then without. This spell works to increase your confidence, health and joy – all the main ingredients of beauty.

What you need:
One of the following crystals: Kunzite, Sodalite, Rhodonite, Honey Opal, Rose Quartz
Athame

Let's begin...

When casting, wear something red or have a large red object nearby, such as a rug or a sheet.

Cast your circle. Stand by your altar, upright with a strong, confident posture.

If you want to, call upon your spirit guide(s) to join and assist you.

"I ask that my guides and angels join me for this session, and assist me in building a strong self-confidence and a positive outlook in life."

Breathe deeply and relax. With every outbreath, feel your tensions and stresses leave you. Allow your thoughts to run, without paying attention to them. Maintain your strong posture.

Take your athame and point it to the ground, and say:

"I absorb Earth's balance and vitality."

Hold the athame against your chest, and feel the solid power of the Earth overflow you, balancing you and making you healthy and vibrant.

Then point the athame to the sky.

"I absorb the power and playfulness of Wind."

Hold the athame against your chest and feel the mighty power of winds fill you. Feel gentle breezes, playful gusts and raging storms within you.

Relax for a moment. Now take your stone and hold it to your Solar Plexus. Say:

"I charge my Solar Plexus
Let fire burn within
From now I will feel comfort
When living in my skin"

Repeat this a few times while you imagine the stone lighting up your chest, filling you with a warm yellow light of strength and confidence, like the Sun burning within you.

Then hold the stone to your Third Eye and say:

"Sun and Moon, shine your light
Grant me now with all your might
Endless beauty for all to sight
It is done – so mote it be."

Repeat a few times, whilst visualising the stone melting all over your head, immersing you in warm, soft oil.

Thank the spirits and close the ceremony. Keep the stone near you in the following weeks while you feel yourself becoming more and more confident, joyful and beautiful.

Spell breakdown

This spell is crafted to bring beauty from within to without; thus focusing on increasing confidence, health and joy.

Kunzite, Sodalite, Rhodonite, Honey Opal are all crystals that increase confidence and personal power.

Rose Quartz promotes love and self-love.

Solar Plexus is the chakra where confidence and self-worth reside.

Athame is used to direct energy; it can be replaced by a wand or any type of knife, unless you want to just use your arm.

Red is a colour of fire, power and sexuality – surround yourself with red and soon you will be entraining to its fiery vibration and move more confidently through life.

Third Eye is the chakra of your inner vision and spirituality – you charge it so that you will see your own beauty.

Intuition Spell

Your intuition is your personal guide towards your highest path. This is how your Higher Self and Spirit Guides communicate with you and lead you in the best possible direction. It is therefore important that you listen to your gut feelings, particularly in the days and weeks after casting a spell.

So how do you know what is true intuition? This spell will help you distinguish higher messages – it creates a talisman that will increase your sensitivity and give you clearer guidance.

What you need:
1 small pouch (purple if you have one)
1 clear quartz crystal
1 amethyst
5 purple candles
1 small piece of paper and a pen
Sandalwood incense

Let's begin…

Start by placing the five candles around you in a circle. As you light the candles, invoke the Spirits and ask for protection and connection during the casting of this spell.

Sit in the middle of your circle. Light the incense. Breathe deeply and relax into a meditation, with your palms open to receive the Universe's energies. Place your attention on your third eye. You are going into your Higher Self to receive a symbol that represents your higher wisdom. Set this intention as you visualise your mind climbing from your third eye out through your crown and higher up, to a place about 1 meter (3 feet) above your head. This is your tenth chakra, where your Higher Self resides.

Go into this place, feel your mind merging with this chakra. Breathe, relax, let it flow. When you are ready, say out loud or in your mind:

"For clearer sight, for clearer mind
A symbol of myself I'll find"

Repeat this a few times, then slowly move your mind back down into your third eye. Once there, you will see a symbol. It can be anything at all. As soon as you see it, draw it on your piece of paper. This symbol represents your higher wisdom and your Higher Self.

Place the piece of paper, together with the quartz and the amethyst, in your pouch, as you say the following words:

"Universe, Spirits, Angels and Guides
Receive my eternal gratitude for all that is
I ask for clearer guidance, as I will listen with a sharper ear
May this talisman heighten my intuition
To receive your messages more clearly
Thank you – so mote it be"

Close your circle by blowing out the candles. Thank the Spirits for their presence. Keep the talisman with you, and keep it under your pillow at night.

If ever you are confused about certain messages or a specific situation, remember your symbol and meditate with your talisman. The best way to receive clear messages is to silence our minds – simply sit with your talisman and open your heart and soul to the never-ending guidance of the Universe, and the answers will come to you.

Spell breakdown

Purple candles are highly spiritual and promote inner peace, wisdom and higher psychic sensitivity. They relax you and open up your inner vision.

Purple (pouch) promotes psychic abilities, psychic power, spirituality and connecting to spirits and deities.

Quartz crystal increases psychic powers and magickal strength.

Amethyst increases spiritual awareness and connection.

Symbols are a powerful way for your Higher Self and higher beings around you to communicate with you – due to subconscious associations, a symbol can hold so much more information than words.

Sandalwood incense is burnt in rituals to increase spiritual awareness and invoke friendly spirits.

Abundance and Prosperity Spell

This is a slightly more complex spell, which is constructed to release any blockages that are holding you back from receiving abundance into your life. It is a three-step process that will open up new possibilities in your life and bring you abundance and prosperity.

What you need:
A green candle
A coin
Pen and paper
A fireproof dish

Let's begin…

Find a place where you can be undisturbed. Sit down and relax. Breathe deeply into your stomach; feel yourself relaxing more and more for each breath. Let a complete calm slowly wash over you.

First, consecrate your candle, or hold the candle in your hand for a while and feel yourself connecting with it. Ask it to help you with your money magick. Then light it, and place the coin next to it.

Remember that, as with everything else, money is just energy floating around. Know that you can begin to allow it to float into your life whenever you want.

Step 1: Releasing the blockages and limiting beliefs around money

First, use your pen and paper to write down what beliefs you may hold that might be blocking you from drawing money into your life – some examples:

~ There is a limited amount of money available in the world
~ Making money is hard
~ I may not be able to pay my bills next month
~ If I don't get this job / if I don't sell enough, then I won't get money (by believing that money can only come from one or two sources, you automatically block off other possible ways of income)

Any negative thoughts around the subject of money that you constantly tell yourself is a limiting belief. Remember that any limitations are only ever imposed by yourself and your beliefs, so if you can identify these beliefs within you, then you can begin to shift them towards abundance.

Once you have finished your list, read through it a few times and try to see how, by subconsciously telling yourself these things every day, you have actually limited yourself. Now that you see them clearly listed in front of you, whenever they pop up in your mind from now on, you will recognise them as limiting beliefs, and you will instead shift your focus towards abundance in order to create more helpful thoughts and beliefs.

Now burn the piece of paper with the green candle, and place it in your fireproof dish. Watch it burn up and feel all those limiting beliefs within you beginning to release.

Step 2: Shifting your focus towards abundance

Now you are ready to cast your circle of protection. Once cast, say:

"In this space I am protected and free
Safe in divine light – so mote it be"

If you want to attract more money into your life, you must begin by focusing on what you already have. Take your pen and paper now, and write down everything you can think of in your life that provides you with money, comfort and security.

Write anything you like that makes you feel happy and grateful – for example, basic things like having a roof over your head, food on the table, and safe place to sleep; and further, any other things you have already created in your life, anything nice you own, any gifts or help you have received from friends and loved ones, etc. By focusing on gratitude towards what you already have, you automatically send a high-vibration energy towards what you want.

To create new, abundant beliefs around money, it will help greatly if you can:

~ Feel excited about money – about having it, spending it, about other people having it
~ Trust that there is enough for you
~ Be happy for other people who have money
~ Feel joy about the things you will buy when you can afford them
~ Be grateful for anything you have in your life, and any gifts or financial help you may receive
~ When you pay bills, instead of thinking about the money you are paying, think about the things you are paying for – i.e. feel grateful that you have electricity, a home etc.

Step 3: Focus on what you want

Now, your energy is really high – clear from limiting beliefs and grateful for all the wonderful things in your life. Finally, let's focus on what you want to manifest.

Take the coin and hold it in your hand. Imagine that you already had plenty of money easily flowing into your life. What would that feel like? What would you do? What would you buy? As you visualise having complete financial freedom, the coin will absorb this energy and this intention. Feel yourself becoming really excited at the possibilities, as you pour this energy into the coin.

Meditate like this for a while – the longer you can stay in this joyful vibration, the better. As you hold this focus, your energies are already beginning to attract more money into your life.

When you feel satisfied, finish by saying:

"Goddess of abundance, God of growth
My friends and allies; I'll gain from you both
Thank you"

Thank the Spirits for their presence and assistance. Blow out the candle. You can keep your gratitude list, to read it again and add more things to it whenever you wish.

Keep the coin and meditate with it, or take it out once a day to remind yourself to let go of the limiting beliefs, and keep bringing yourself into the higher vibration of abundance and possibilities. Keep visualising a life of financial freedom, and do so joyfully and hopefully, knowing that it will be yours.

Spell breakdown

Limiting beliefs are released to make way for a more helpful focus on money.

Green is the colour of growth and prosperity, and it is also the colour of the Goddess, who is always ready and willing to bring you abundance and joy.

The coin is a powerful representation of money.

Be Here Now: Mindfulness Spell

Being present in the moment allows you to fully appreciate and enjoy every experience, and it helps you stay calm and composed during tough times. But the main reason that I bring it up here is because regular meditation and mindfulness practice will increase your magick powers infinitely. With a clear, calm and focused mind you can direct your energies wherever you like. You can release blockages and steer your life in any direction that takes your fancy. In this state, the sky truly is the limit!

If you wish to become more mindful in your life, this spell will help you on your journey.

What you need:
5 small candles or tea lights (preferably white)
Incense: Cardamom or Lemongrass
A piece of paper cut into the shape of a body (25-30cm long), with your name and birthdate written on it
1 Smoky Quartz crystal

Let's begin...

Light the incense and cast your circle.

Place the paper shape in front of you, and place the candles by its head, feet and hands. Leave them unlit for now, and relax into a meditative state. Focus on your breathing, in and out through your nose, deep into your stomach. Become aware of your body.

Now light the two candles at the paper body's feet. Sit back into meditation, close your eyes, and focus your mind on your feet. Feel the flame bringing them to life, feel the heat trickle in through your feet and up your legs as you focus entirely on this part of your body. If a thought enters your head, simply let it go and bring your attention back to your feet. Notice how your feet and legs feel – the temperature, the air or fabric against the skin, the way the foot divides into five toes... It's amazing how much you can feel when you put your mind to it.

You have now brought your feet and legs into the present.

Next, light the candles by its hands and do the same thing. With your eyes closed, visualise the fire awakening your hands and arms, bringing them fully into the Now. Notice how they feel. Are they comfortable? Relaxed? Warm, cool? Become fully aware of your hands and arms, not by touching them but simply by feeling them with your full awareness. You may feel they begin to tingle.

Carry on like this until you feel content. You have now brought your hands and arms into the present.

Finally, we will bring your mind and heart into the present. Light the candle by the paper doll's head. Say:

"Spirits and Guardians who guide and protect me
Help me stay mindful and ever-present
To bring my focus into now, to notice all that is
To appreciate each moment with inner calm and peace
Thank you"

Lie down and place your Smoky Quartz on your third eye.

Now do the same, but with your eyes open. The flame is calling your mind into the now, into a quiet and focused observation of the present moment. Feel yourself being fully inside your body. Notice the temperature, the feeling of your clothes against your skin, the weight of the crystal on your forehead. What do you see around you? What can you smell?

If your mind strays, simply take a deep breath and gently bring your focus back into your body. Feel the five candles surrounding you like a circle of wakefulness, a fire that binds you to the moment. Lie here for as long as you want.

When you're ready, take your crystal in your hand and sit up. Say:

"I charge this crystal with my awareness and presence
So it may ground and center me whenever I need
To keep me in the moment, for joy and full experience
With the help of my blessed spirits, may I succeed!"

Close your circle. Keep your crystal with you whenever you want – keep it near you to ground and center you, and meditate with it to promote focus and mindfulness.

Whenever you feel yourself becoming scatter-minded, anxious, stressed or depressed, close your eyes for a moment and visualise the five candle flames burning around your body, and feel yourself once again being entirely within your body and in the moment, where there is only awareness and joy.

Spell breakdown

Cardamom is burned for mental clarity, concentration, confidence, courage, enthusiasm and motivation.

Lemongrass is burn for mental clarity and will bring you into the present.

Smoky Quartz is a Root Chakra stone, grounding and centering; it calms the mind, eases fear, enhances energies, and lifts your mood.

Silver Lining: Spell to See the Positive

Sometimes life deals us hard blows. It's not all meant to be a smooth ride; we are here to learn and grow. But in the midst of a problem or crisis it can be easy to forget that there is a positive aspect to every situation. No matter how difficult or sad things get, there is always a silver lining.

This spell is cast to help you gain perspective and find the positive in any situation.

What you need:
5 blue candles
Angelica incense

Let's begin...

Place the five candles in a circle (one for each Element and one for Spirit). Light the Angelica and open your circle, then sit down in the middle.

Feel the Angelica connect you with your Higher Self and spiritual source. Then address the Goddess and God:

"Goddess and God, Mother and Father
The two sides of the coin
Remind me of duality
Remind me of polarity
Night and day
Land and sea
Life and death

In my stride there is reward
Bring me clarity to see
Bring me strength to move forward
So mote it be"

Now relax into a meditation. Focus your attention on your third eye – the seat of clarity and spirituality, and your ability to see different perspectives and grasp the bigger picture. Visualise it opening up like a flower, shining a bright, violet light. Feel it expanding, filling the room.

In this peaceful, clear state, consider your situation without judgement. Ask yourself, what is good about this situation? What good can come of it? What is the positive aspect? Then relax and let the answers come to you. Give it some time, and see how you feel. Don't force it.

If it doesn't come to you straightaway, ask that the silver lining appear to you as and when you are ready.

Close your circle.

Spell breakdown

Angelica is burned for protection, harmony, integration, insight and understanding, stability and meditation.

Third eye is where your spirituality and inner vision reside, and your ability to see the bigger picture.

Blue candles are used in rituals to obtain wisdom and inner peace. It helps you see and express the truth, as well as lifts you to a more joyful frame of mind. It promotes protection, understanding, health and joy.

Good Luck Spell

When we try to accomplish or attract something new into our lives, it is important to put in the focus and the work. However, it can be helpful to give things a nudge in our favour.

This is a good luck spell to help things along for you to achieve success.

This spell can be cast any time, but will be enhanced during a waxing or full moon.

What you need:
Frankincense
3 candles – orange or gold
Pen and paper

Let's begin...

Cast your circle and light the incense.

Place the candles in a triangle for luck, but do not light them yet.

Say the following words:

"Goddess and God, Spirits and Guides
Thank you for all that I have
I ask you now for [whatever it is you want]
Aid me as I work to achieve it
Please bring it to me when the time is right
So mote it be"

Now visualise what your life would be like if you already had this thing you wish for. Really soak yourself in the feeling of good luck, success, joy, achievement. Feel the elation in your chest, and hold on to that feeling. Meditate on it as you go deeper into yourself. An image or symbol will now appear in your inner vision. This symbol contains the energy of your wish. As soon as you see it, draw it on your piece of paper.

Now place the paper with the symbol within the triangle of candles.

As you light each candle, say:

"Fire, ignite my dream, for the highest good."

Sit with the lit candles and visualise good luck coming your way. Trust that the Universe will bring what is best for you. Immerse yourself in gratitude towards life and all that the Goddess and God have already brought you.

Then take your piece of paper and bury it in the earth (or in a plant pot) as you say:

"Earth, seal my dream, for the highest good."

Note that this spell will bring precisely what is best for you – however, it may come in unexpected forms. Remember to keep an open mind and an open heart and look out for opportunities and signs.

Spell breakdown

Frankincense attracts good luck, protects against negativity and evil, and instils courage.

Triangle / number 3 represents the triple aspect of the Goddess/God; symbolises creativity, activity, growth and results; expression and communication; enthusiasm and appreciation.

Orange candles are burned for luck, stimulation and energy; control, personal strength and power. They also help bring flexibility and adaptability in new situations.

Gold candles are used to call upon luck and financial gain, to instil intuition and confidence, and is said to attract the influences of higher forces.

Earth is a material element that will help manifest your spell into the physical realm.

Spell to Get Rid of Bad Habits

Whatever bad habits you would like to kick, you always have the strength and willpower within you to stay focused and release them. This spell is constructed to bring that willpower to the surface and activate it so that you can stay calm and focused whilst ridding yourself of any behavioural patterns you're not fond of.

What you need
A black candle
Sage incense
1 piece of Iron Pyrite (Fool's Gold)
Garlic

Let's begin...

Cast your circle.

Light the candle and incense in front of you. As the sage fills the room, feel it filling and cleansing you and the space around you. Think of your bad habit now – but don't judge it, simply observe it and its patterns. It's something you have been doing, and now you will release it, so no negative thoughts or feelings are necessary (or helpful) here. As you gently focus on your habit, watch and smell the incense and allow it to immerse your bad habit, to purify and release it. Imagine the black candle burning away your old patterns.

Take your iron pyrite and hold it in your hands. Say:

"Iron Pyrite, do your deed
Awaken in me the strength I need
A focused mind; a soul aligned
Time to leave this habit behind!"

Imagine now how you will think/feel/act when you have shed this bad habit. What good will come of it? How will you feel? Think of the satisfaction of being rid of it once and for all. As you visualise this improved you, feel the iron pyrite coming alive in your hands as it is charged with your energies.

Now, address your Higher Self and Spirit Guides, to ask for their help along the way. Do this in whatever way feels comfortable to you – be it through a prayer, or speaking to them as you would to a friend. Tell them how you wish to be (without the bad habit) and ask that they help you stay focused and strong, so that you can make this happen. Ask them to remind you *why* you want to get rid of the habit, so that you can keep this image in your mind should you feel yourself slipping back into old patterns again.

Finally, take the garlic and charge it with the same image you placed inside the iron pyrite, and then hang the garlic over your bed or somewhere in your house where you spend a lot of time.

Close your circle and thank the spirits for their presence and assistance. Blow out the candle.

Keep the iron pyrite with you everywhere, and when you feel tempted to go back to the old habit, simply take out the iron pyrite and connect with the visualisation you charged it with.

Spell breakdown

Black candles are used to help let go of old habits. They also banish negativity and increase your inner strength and self-control.

Sage is a cleansing herb that protects against bad influences and purifies the self. It strengthens your mental focus and heals the soul.

Iron Pyrite (Fool's Gold) strengthens willpower and instils positive thinking, making it the perfect stone for this type of spell. It also helps awaken your inner potential, whilst balancing and increasing your energy and protecting you from negative influences.

Garlic heals, protects, purifies, and cleanses. When hung in your home, it will help to increase your mental strength and willpower.

Spell to Overcome a Difficult Past

We all carry baggage from our past, baggage that might be weighing us down unless we release it. No matter what suffering you have gone through in your life, it can be overcome and there is always something to be learned from it. No suffering happens without reason. This spell will help you gain some perspective, release your past grief and move forward into a lighter and more joyful existence.

What you need:
Pen and paper
1 white candle
5 green candles
Fireproof dish
Incense: Cedarwood or Sage

Let's begin...

First, light your incense.

Sit with your pen and paper ready, and bring all those painful memories to the surface. Either work on them one by one, or treat them as one big collection of memories that you want to release. Think of all the hurt and the pain, feel it manifesting as physical sensations in your body. Usually we don't allow ourselves to *feel* this way, but that is the only way to truly release your emotions – by acknowledging and honouring them.

Turn your attention fully to the memories, without fear or judgement – remember, no matter what thoughts or feelings arise now, you are safe in this space. Nothing can hurt you here, and for each emotion you allow yourself to *really feel*, you will become increasingly lighter and more hopeful. The only way out is the way through, so let's get started!

When you feel all those big negative emotions accumulating inside you, take your pen and paper and free-write anything that comes to mind. Write about the memories, about how they felt then, how they feel now, any anger you may hold towards others – anything that needs to be let out. Write without stopping or thinking, just let it flow. Get your blood boiling, feel all those horrible emotions, let all those painful memories spill onto the page. As the words pour out of you, so does the hurt you have been carrying.

When you feel yourself calming down a bit, and the words stop flowing, then put your pen down and take a few deep breaths to relax.

With all this negativity released, you are now ready to cast your circle. Place the five green candles around it to mark out the points of a pentagram, but leave them unlit for now. Place the white candle in front of you and light it.

Now place the paper(s) you wrote on over the flame of the white candle and say:

"Fire, burn these thoughts away
Flame, release my hurt and pain
White, purify my soul
Spirits, lead me to my goal"

Let the paper burn to ashes in the fireproof dish. Watch it go up in flames and visualise your past transforming along with it. Feel all your hurt releasing, and your heart and soul becoming light and joyful. Breathe deeply and imagine that for each out-breath you let go of old, unwanted things, and for each in-breath you take in fresh air and new beginnings.

Now that you have released your hurt and pain, you will use the Goddess and the colour green to rejuvenate you and charge you with hope and love. Move clockwise along the circle, lighting the candles one by one, as you say:

"With green and flame I invoke the Goddess, and the element of Earth."
"With green and flame I invoke the Goddess, and the element of Air."
"With green and flame I invoke the Goddess, and the element of Fire."
"With green and flame I invoke the Goddess, and the element of Water."
"With green and flame I invoke the Goddess, and Spirit."

Then lie down in the middle, with your head next to the Spirit candle, and each of your arms and legs pointing out to the other candles. Say:

"Let new beginnings come to me
Finally a chance to see
A past released, a life renewed
Let old be old and new be new"

Now lie there and feel the power of the incantation do its work. Feel the magick of the green candles streaming into you through your legs, arms and head, converging in the middle around your solar plexus and heart, filling your entire being with a healing green light. Keep yourself floating in this warm, happy state for as long as you want. The longer you can joyfully remain in this feeling, the better. When you feel ready, say:

"Mother Goddess, thank you for setting me free
I look forward now with hope and joy – so mote it be"

Close your circle and blow out the candles. Leave the incense to burn to the end. Thank the Goddess, Spirits, and Elements for their presence and assistance.

Spell breakdown

Cedarwood is burned for healing, grounding and balance. It purifies and releases negative baggage, brings clarity and wisdom to any situation, and insight that will help you see the positive in what you have been through.

Sage promotes healing of the body, mind and soul, and also purifies and protects against negativity.

White candles hold a combination of all colours, which makes them balanced and pure. They promote purification, tranquillity and peace.

Green candles connect to the Goddess and the Earth, promoting love, renewal, rejuvenation, and good fortune. They also bring you closer to the spirit of nature.

Cleansing Ritual

Every day our energy fields are being interfered with by people, events, and even our own thoughts. Negative energy can attach to us and block our flow, which can bring us down, cause irritation and drain our vitality. It's important to keep ourselves in check to make sure we are not being too affected by this. Eating well, exercising, spending time in nature and meditating are all good ways to restore our energy flow and stay balanced, but sometimes we need a little extra help.

This cleansing ritual can be performed at any time when you're feeling low, tired or otherwise affected by negativity.

(If you find yourself in a hurry, you can go directly to Steps 2 and 3.)

What you need:
Air: Sage incense
Fire: A silver/grey candle
Earth: Sea salt
Water: Chalice filled with water

Cast your circle, then light the incense and the candle.

Meditate for a few minutes while the sage fills the room. Each time you breathe out, relax a little more. The more relaxed you are, the better your energies flow, and the easier it is to release any unwanted negativity.

When you feel calm and ready you may begin.

Step 1: Element cleanse

Hold your hands over the incense and say, *"with air I cleanse myself."* Let the smoke twirl around your fingers for a few moments. Feel the cleansing properties of sage immerse you; imagine air clearing and refreshing you.

Then hold your hands above the candle (at a safe distance) and say, *"with fire I cleanse myself."* Visualise the flame burning away anything unwanted within you; transforming you.

Now take the sea salt and crumble it between your fingers, gently rubbing it on your hands, and say, *"with earth I cleanse myself."* Feel the solidity and stability of earth, grounding you and healing you.

Then dip your hands in the water, again gently rubbing your hands, and say *"with water I cleanse myself."* Visualise fresh spring water flowing through your body, cleansing you and gently leading you to a better place.

Sit in silence for a moment while you let the elements do their work.

Step 2: Releasing negativity

The most effective way of releasing negative entities and energies (unless they are unusually powerful) is to firmly ask them to leave.

Go inside yourself, become completely aware of your body, and say the following:

"Any energy that no longer serves me, please leave now. Thank you for your presence. Now I am sending you home."

Say it with conviction, firmly but lovingly. Keep repeating it, and pay attention to any feelings in your body. As you say these words, negativity will shed from you like the skin off a snake. If you're sensitive you may feel a pulling sensation or a feeling of suddenly becoming lighter.

Repeat until you intuitively feel done (this can be 5 times or 50 times, anything that feels right for you.)

(For a more in-depth explanation of this process, see the aura-clearing exercise on page 73).

Step 3: Filling with light

This step is vital: after releasing the negative energies you will have holes in your aura which must be filled with light. Otherwise other negative energy can easily latch on to you and you'll have to start the process again.

Visualise your crown (the top of your head) opening up, like a funnel going from the heavens into your body. Visualise pulling down divine light that will fill every gap in your aura as you repeat the words:

"I ask that my energy body is filled with pure healing light."

Repeat a few times, then thank the spirits and elements, and close your circle.

During the rest of the day/evening, whenever it comes to mind, visualise your open crown and the light flowing into you.

Banishing and Protection Spell

If you find yourself being attacked or otherwise influenced by an otherworldly spirit or entity, you must seek protection. This is a three-stage process to rid yourself of any unwanted beings.

1. Protection

If you can, acquire one or more of the following gemstones:

- ~ Black Tourmaline
- ~ Agate
- ~ Bloodstone
- ~ Emerald
- ~ Labradorite
- ~ Black Onyx
- ~ Peridot
- ~ Emerald

These are crystals that protect you from harmful spirits and psychic intrusion. Black Tourmaline may be the most effective, but any of them would work. You can also use orgonite containing one of these stones.

The next step will be to surround yourself with a shield of protective light. This comes from within, and you can conjure it up yourself through meditation.

Begin each day by sitting down in a quiet space for five minutes, visualising a bright bubble of light around you, reaching about an arm's length away from your body. Make it any colour you feel comfortable with.

Repeat the following words: *"I surround myself with a shield of protection. I am safe within my space."* Feel the light emanating from you, growing brighter with each deep breath. It is strong and controlled, vibrating at a high frequency. No evil spirit can penetrate this force field.

Finally, ask your spirit guides, guardian angels and the Goddess and God to protect you.

2. Cleansing

You will then need to cleanse the space where you sense the negative intrusion. If it follows you around, use these methods around your body.

Palo Santo is a holy South American wood, which the shamans use to drive out evil spirits. You can buy this online for pennies, and it lasts for ages. If you can get hold of Palo Santo, burn some now, or otherwise use sage, sandalwood or frankincense. Sprinkle sea salt around the area. Repeat the following words:

"Any energy that doesn't serve me, please leave now.
You don't belong here. I am sending you home.
Thank you."

Say these words, or variations of this nature, until you feel satisfied.

3. Communication

Follow steps 1 and 2. If they don't work, you must try to communicate with the spirit. This can be dangerous, so follow the instructions carefully.

Cast a protective circle. Sprinkle sea salt around it for extra protection.

Wear or carry your gemstones or orgonites. Ask them to protect you.

Activate your protective light shield as per step 1.

Then you may speak to the spirit. Say something along the lines of:

"Spirit who presently resides here. I am protected and you cannot harm me. I address you with the utmost respect.

"I do not know your reasons for being here, but you are intruding on my/our live(s), and there is nothing for you here. I am asking you to please leave. Go back whence you came. Go home, where you will be at peace. Thank you."

When you're ready, close your circle.

Keep your gemstones or orgonites near you as often as you can. Whenever you feel like there might be a negative presence, take deep breaths (this strengthens your aura), try to remain calm, visualise the light bubble around you, and ask your guides/angels to stay near and keep you safe.

If this still doesn't work, you should contact a psychic for assistance.

New Beginnings:
Ritual to Welcome the New Year

Though calendars are a human creation and differ throughout the world, the cycle of life is a constant and New Year is a powerful time to say goodbye to what has been and set our intentions for what is to come. Here is a ritual with which we give thanks for what we have and steer our lives towards what we want.

Samhain is traditionally known as the Witch's New Year, so you can perform this ritual in the days or nights leading up to either Samhain or your calendar New Year's Eve.

What you need:
Pen and paper
Incense (preferably sage or citronella)
1 black candle
1 chalice and water
1 quartz crystal of any size
1 small jar

Sit or stand somewhere quiet and comfortable where you can create a holy space to perform this ritual (or by your altar if you have one). Focus on your breathing, calm your mind and soul, and when you feel relaxed and at peace, you may begin.

Write on the piece of paper briefly what you intend for the coming year. Are you looking for love, financial stability, friendship, joy, adventure? Write briefly and generally – the Universe will bring what is best for you, so it is best not to focus too much on specifics, but it is a good sign if you get a warm, fuzzy feeling of excitement while writing it!

Then let us begin. We engage the elements one by one.

Air: Light incense, ideally sage (for cleansing) or citronella (for cleansing and healing). As it fills the space around you, let it surround and cleanse your being. Remember and honour the ever-changing nature of air, and know that you will approach change with an open and optimistic mind. Say:

"Goddess and God, Mother and Father
I give my thanks for all that I have
With air I cleanse the past
To prepare for a prosperous new year
For the highest good
So be it"

Let the incense fill the air as you allow any negativity or heaviness leave your energy field. Visualise a bright rainbow around you, growing ever brighter and more colourful with every breath.

"Thank you."

Fire: Light a black candle (to clear negativity and gain strength and self-control). As you light the candle, contemplate what you have been through in the past year, and focus on releasing any energy baggage you may be carrying, disintegrating it through the transforming fire; then visualise the fire bringing energy and spark to your future. Say:

"Goddess and God, Mother and Father
I give my thanks for all that I have
With fire I ignite the future
To prepare for a prosperous new year
For the highest good
So be it"

Leave the candle burning until you have finished the ritual.

"Thank you."

Water: Take the chalice and fill it with water. Cup your hands around the chalice and sit with it, allowing your energies to merge and blend with those of the water. Fill your heart with gratitude for water, its purifying and life-giving properties. Recognise the aspects of water within you; your ability to flow around obstacles and find the path of least resistance. Raise the chalice and say:

"Goddess and God, Mother and Father
I give my thanks for all that I have
With water I vitalise the future

To prepare for a prosperous new year
For the highest good
So be it"

Drink the water. Pay close attention to the feeling of it in your body, cleansing, reviving, energising.

"Thank you."

Earth: Take the piece of paper and wrap it around the quartz, which will assist in manifesting your wishes. Feel the stability and strength; the everlasting presence of Mother Earth. Know that your desires will materialise in the best possible way. Hold it in your hands and say:

"Goddess and God, Mother and Father
I give my thanks for all that I have
With earth I manifest my wishes
To prepare for a prosperous new year
For the highest good
So be it"

Place it in the jar and keep somewhere safe and undisturbed.

"Thank you."

Now thank the elements for their presence and assistance, and send them on their way by patting the floor/ground three times.

Spend some time visualising already having manifested your wishes on the piece of paper. Feel the butterflies of joy or the calm of satisfaction fill you. Hold on to that feeling as you close the ritual and move into the New Year.

Body Appreciation Prayer

This is an incantation which can be read any time, to remind yourself to love and appreciate your body and the gift of life.

My body is my temple, my soul resides within
It works in perfect harmony beneath my precious skin
No matter size or shape I am, no matter looks or age
I love myself and all I am; my body at each stage

It keeps me here so I can hear, and see, and feel each day
So I can barefoot walk in grass, and dance around in rain
Mother Goddess, Father God, beneath your loving gaze
I'll love and cherish all I am, until the end of days

Afterword

I very much enjoyed writing this book, and I hope it was as enjoyable for you to read. Hopefully you have gained some new knowledge and useful insights that will assist you not only in your magick, but also in your everyday life.

You may find that you want to return to the book and re-read certain chapters, since its contents will seem different to you once you have absorbed and adopted the practices contained in it, and you will find new aspects and angles to the information given.

Certainly, that is how I approach my development as a witch, and as a human being – we are constantly growing and learning, and every day we are new and fresh; a clean slate upon which we can create the person we want to be. It is never too late to change or improve ourselves, in order to attain our goals and create the most wonderful and magickal lives we can possibly imagine.

I am hoping this book will be a helpful guide on your journey.

Thank you for reading – and to those of you who are members of the Wiccan Spells community, I want to offer my warmest thanks for your continued support and participation. This book is for you.

Blessed Be,

Amaris

Stay in touch – find me online:

Website: www.wiccanspells.info
Facebook: www.facebook.com/freewiccanspells
Twitter: twitter.com/AmarisSilver